VOLUME **1**

GROWING in Jesus

Becoming More Like Jesus by Studying His Life

The greatest power in the universe
to draw people to Jesus
is an understanding of His love
as revealed in His life.
—Mark and Ernestine Finley

VOLUME **1**

GROWING in Jesus

Becoming More Like Jesus by Studying His Life

Mark and Ernestine Finley

Pacific Press®
Publishing Association
Nampa, Idaho | www.pacificpress.com

Cover design by Gerald Lee Monks
Cover design resources from Goodsalt | Phil McKay
Inside design by Gerald Lee Monks and Aaron Troia

p. 3 © Goodsalt—Phil McKay, p. 6 © Goodsalt—Phil McKay, p. 12 © Goodsalt—Lars Justinen, p. 15 © Goodsalt—Justinen Creative, p. 18, 64, 91, 92, 107, 122, 148, 175, 189—Lightstock, p. 23, 38, 55, 69, 81, 83, 103, 109, 115, 116, 125, 130, 132, 137, 146, 153, 165, 177, 191—Gettyimages, p. 24 © Goodsalt—Lars Justinen, p. 29 © Goodsalt—Michael Agliolo, p. 31 © Review and Herald Publishing—artist unknown, p. 40 © Goodsalt—Lars Justinen, p. 42 © Review and Herald Publishing—Raoul Vitale, p. 48 © Review and Herald Publishing—Raoul Vitale, p. 51 © Review and Herald Publishing—Raoul Vitale, p. 56 © Goodsalt—Lars Justinen, p. 61 © Goodsalt—Steve Creitz, p. 66 © Goodsalt—Lars Justinen, p. 70 © Goodsalt—Lars Justinen, p. 75 © Review and Herald Publishing—Russ Harlan, p. 78 © Goodsalt—Kevin Carden, p. 84 © Goodsalt—Lars Justinen, p. 89 © Goodsalt—Kevin Carden, p. 96 © Pacific Press Publishing—John Steel, p. 100 © Goodsalt—Lifeway Collection, p. 106 © Goodsalt—Lars Justinen, p. 110 © Goodsalt—Lars Justinen, p. 118 © Goodsalt—Lars Justinen, p. 126 © Goodsalt—Lars Justinen, p. 134 © Goodsalt—Justinen Creative, p. 138 © Pacific Press Publishing—Lars Justinen, p. 143 © Review and Herald Publishing—artist unknown, p. 154 © Goodsalt—Lars Justinen, p. 159 © Goodsalt—Lifeway Collection, p. 162 © Goodsalt—Phil McKay, p. 166 © Pacific Press Publishing—John Steel, p. 170 © Goodsalt—Phil McKay, p. 178 © Goodsalt—Lars Justinen, p. 182 © Pacific Press Publishing—artist unknown, p. 187 © Goodsalt—Lars Justinen

The authors assume full responsibility for the accuracy of all facts and quotations as cited in this book.

Unless otherwise noted, all Scripture is taken from the New King James Version®. Copyright © 1982 by Thomas Nelson. Used by permission. All rights reserved.

Scripture quotations marked AMP are taken from the Amplified® Bible, copyright © 2015 by The Lockman Foundation. Used by permission. (www.Lockman.org)

Scripture quotations marked KJV are from the King James Version.

Scriptures quoted from RSV are from the Revised Standard Version of the Bible, copyright © 1946, 1952, 1971 by the Division of Christian Education of the National Council of the Churches of Christ in the U.S.A. Used by permission.

Scripture quotations marked *Weymouth* are taken from The Weymouth New Testament. The Weymouth New Testament is in the public domain.

Purchase additional copies of this book by calling toll-free 1-800-765-6955 or by visiting AdventistBookCenter.com.

Library of Congress Cataloging-in-Publication Data

Names: Finley, Mark, 1945– author. | Finley, Ernestine, author.
Title: Growing in Jesus / Mark and Ernestine Finley.
Description: Nampa, Idaho : Pacific Press Publishing Association, 2020– | Summary: "A series of Bible studies about growing in knowledge of and relationship with Jesus"—Provided by publisher.
Identifiers: LCCN 2020016031 | ISBN 9780816366767 (v. 1 ; paperback)
Subjects: LCSH: Jesus Christ—Person and offices—Biblical teaching—Textbooks.
Classification: LCC BT207 .F565 2020 | DDC 232—dc23
LC record available at https://lccn.loc.gov/2020016031

June 2020

CONTENTS

INTRODUCTION

Becoming More Like Jesus by Studying His Life

Volume 1 of *Growing in Jesus* contains a series of interactive, inspirational lessons on the life of Christ. The chapters cover Christ's birth, ministry, death, resurrection, high priestly intercession, and second coming. In this series, Jesus is exalted as our all-powerful Creator, loving Redeemer, interceding High Priest, and coming King.

The chapters are intentionally designed to lead each participant into a deeper relationship and closer fellowship with Jesus. While the Bible is primary throughout the lessons, the modern gift of prophecy, as manifested in the writings of Ellen White, gives added insight into each subject. These prophetic revelations provide a depth of understanding, a richness of meaning, and a broad comprehension of the life of Christ.

Studying His life, we are charmed by His love, moved to our core by His sacrifice, and motivated by His example to totally commit our lives to His service.

This may be used as a midweek Bible-study series in local congregations, as a pastor's Sabbath-morning Bible class, or a follow-up seminar to evangelistic meetings. It can also easily be used in individual Bible studies or small home groups. Many pastors will find it helpful in anchoring recently baptized converts in their newfound faith.

Jesus promised, "And I, if I am lifted up from the earth, will draw all peoples to Myself" (John 12:32).

The reason we have written these lessons is that we profoundly believe Jesus' words. The greatest power in the universe to draw people to Jesus is an understanding of His love as revealed in His life. It is our prayer that as you study these lessons, reflect on His life, and understand more completely His love, you will be amazed by a new appreciation of His character and be drawn to Him in new, remarkable ways.

May your life be forever changed as you study these pages.
Mark and Ernestine Finley

LESSON

Jesus, the Eternal, Everlasting God

Jesus has become quite popular these days. Country-and-western stars sing about Him. Popular news magazines feature Him. Victorious athletic teams celebrate Him. Politicians openly confess Him. Hollywood blockbuster movies acclaim Him. Thousands are seeking to discover Him. Religious leaders invite us to follow Him.

- But who is He? Who is this Jesus? Is He worthy of our allegiance?
- Can He really forgive our sins?
- Can He give us victory over undesirable habits?
- Can He change our lives for the better?
- Is His offer of eternal life real?

Throughout this book, you will discover Jesus, who loves you more than you can ever imagine and who has plans for your life beyond your wildest dreams. In following Him, you will find the secret of life's true meaning. If you are already a committed follower of Jesus, this book of lessons will lead you to a deeper experience with Him.

As you study His life, you will sense yourself drawing closer to Him. A new peace will flood your soul; a new joy will fill your life; a new sense of purpose will be yours. Knowing Him better, you will uncover the secret of really living. In this first lesson, "Jesus: The Eternal, Everlasting God," you will discover who Jesus really is.

Jesus declares Himself to be eternal

QUESTION 1 Who is Jesus? Who does He declare Himself to be?

"I am the Alpha and the Omega, the Beginning and the End," says the Lord, "who is and who was and who is to come, the Almighty." . . .

"I am the Alpha and the Omega, the First and the Last," and, "What you see, write in a book and send it to the seven churches which are in Asia: to Ephesus, to Smyrna, to Pergamos, to Thyatira, to Sardis, to Philadelphia, and to Laodicea" (Revelation 1:8, 11).

When John the revelator was an exile on the Isle of Patmos, Jesus reassured him that He is the "Beginning and the End," "the First and the Last." Jesus truly is from everlasting to everlasting. Although this is difficult to comprehend, the good news is, it's true!

In verses 8 and 11, Jesus emphatically declares that He is "the *Alpha* and the *Omega*," "the *Beginning* and the *End*," "the *First* and the *Last*." Jesus had no beginning and will have no end. Jesus Himself says He is the One "*who is* and *who was* and *who is* to come, the Almighty" (emphasis added).

Jesus reveals His divinity

The author of Hebrews tells us that the clearest way that God reveals His character to a fallen planet is through His Son, Jesus. Carefully notice seven significant characteristics of Jesus in the following passage.

God, who at various times and in various ways spoke in time past to the fathers by the prophets, has in these last days spoken to us by His Son, whom He has appointed heir of all things, through whom also He made the worlds; who being the brightness of His glory and the express image of His person, and upholding all things by the word of His power, when He had by Himself purged our sins, sat down at the right hand of the Majesty on high, having become so much better than the angels, as He has by inheritance obtained a more excellent name than they (Hebrews 1:1–4).

- Jesus is *God's channel of communication* (verse 2).
- Jesus is the "*heir of all things*" (verse 2).
- Jesus is the *Creator* (verse 2).
- Jesus is the "*brightness of [God's] glory*" (verse 3).

- Jesus is the "*express image*" of God (verse 3).
- Jesus is the *Sustainer of the universe* (verse 3).
- Jesus is the *great Redeemer* (verse 3).

Of the many titles that the prophet Isaiah gives to Jesus, two reveal His divinity:

For unto us a Child is born,
Unto us a Son is given;
And the government will be upon His
    shoulder.
And His name will be called
Wonderful, Counselor, Mighty God,
Everlasting Father, Prince of Peace"
    (Isaiah 9:6).

He is called the "Mighty God" and the "Everlasting Father."

Jesus, the One who was with God the Father and stood in the councils of the Most High, was the greatest and most wonderful gift that Heaven could give to save humanity. He reveals what God is like, "In the Teacher sent from God, heaven gave to men its best and greatest. He who had stood in the councils of the Most High, who had dwelt in the innermost sanctuary of the Eternal, was the One chosen to reveal in person to humanity the knowledge of God."[1]

The Father addresses Jesus as God in Hebrews 1:8.

But to the Son He says:
    "Your throne, O God, is forever and
        ever;
    A scepter of righteousness is the
        scepter of Your kingdom."

Throughout the New Testament, multiple sources reveal that Jesus is the divine Son of God.

The Bible gives evidence of the divinity of Christ:

- The *Father* declares Him to be God—Hebrews 1:8.
- *Jesus* declares Himself to be God—John 8:58.
- The *angels* declare Him to be God—Luke 2:9–14.
- The *prophets* declare Him to be God—Matthew 1:22, 23; 8:17.
- The *disciples* declare Him to be God—John 20:28; Matthew 16:16.
- The *Jews* declare Him to be God—John 10:33; Luke 5:20, 21.
- The *Roman centurion* declares Him to be God—Matthew 27:54.
- The *demons* declare Him to be God—Mark 5:2–7.

Jesus always existed

Jesus existed from everlasting to everlasting. Throughout all eternity, Jesus was one with the Father. Jesus declared it in His prayer to the Father (John 17:11). And earlier in His ministry, when some Jews challenged Jesus' identity, Jesus declared it in no uncertain terms (John 8:58). John also says that Jesus was with the Father from everlasting to everlasting before the world was created (John 1:1–5). The fact that Jesus always existed is abundantly plain. Whether one believes that Jesus always existed or not, it is still true. All the evidence points to the fact that Jesus is eternal!

Micah, the prophet, recorded God saying that Jesus, the One born in Bethlehem, existed from eternity:

"But you, Bethlehem Ephrathah,
Though you are little among the thousands
    of Judah,
Yet out of you shall come forth to Me
The One to be Ruler in Israel,
Whose goings forth are from old,
From everlasting" (Micah 5:2).

Jesus existed with the Father before the world was created. John records Jesus' prayer: "And now, O Father, glorify Me together with Yourself, with the glory which I had with You before the world was" (John 17:5). Ellen G. White declares, "The Lord Jesus Christ, the divine Son of God, existed from eternity, a distinct person, yet one with the Father."[2]

She adds, "The Son of God shared the Father's throne, and the glory of the eternal, *self-existent One* encircled both."[3] "Self-existent" describes a nature that is not dependent on anything other than itself for its own existence. Christ is eternal and not dependent on any other being in the universe as the source of His life. "Christ was the Son of God; He had been one with Him before the angels were called into existence. He had *ever* stood at the right hand of the Father."[4] Furthermore, "in speaking of His pre-existence, Christ carries the mind back through dateless ages. He assures us that there *never was a time*

when He was not in close fellowship with the eternal God. He . . . had been with God as one brought up with Him."[5]

The Father establishes the eternal nature of Christ by describing Their cooperation in the creation of this world. The author of Hebrews testifies,

"You, LORD, in the beginning laid the
    foundation of the earth,
And the heavens are the work of Your
    hands.
They will perish, but You remain;
And they will all grow old like a garment;
Like a cloak You will fold them up,
And they will be changed.
But You are the same,
And Your years will not fail" (Hebrews
    1:10–12).

Also, "Jesus Christ is the same yesterday, today, and forever" (Hebrews 13:8).

Jesus is God with us

QUESTION **2** What name is given to Jesus in Matthew's Gospel? What does it mean?

" 'Behold, the virgin shall be with child, and bear a Son, and they shall call His name Immanuel,' which is translated, 'God with us' " (Matthew 1:23).

_____

_____

The amazing fact is that Jesus, the everlasting Creator, loves us so much. He cares for us. He longs for us to be with Him where He is. He knows what we face every day and is there to help and guide us. What a God. What a Savior. What a Friend!

Writing about Christ's title Immanuel,

Ellen G. White states, "From the days of eternity the Lord Jesus Christ was one with the Father; He was 'the image of God,' the image of His greatness and majesty, 'the outshining of His glory.' It was to manifest this glory that He came to our world. To this sin-darkened earth He came to reveal the light of God's love,—to be 'God with us.' Therefore it was prophesied of Him, 'His name shall be called Immanuel.' "[6]

There is nothing that parallels this love. His love is shown to us through every doctrine of Scripture. Jesus is love and the Center of every doctrine! The teachings of the Bible are not arbitrary legalistic requirements—they are at the center of God's great unending love.

In truth, "since Jesus came to dwell with us, we know that God is acquainted with our trials, and sympathizes with our griefs. Every son and daughter of Adam may understand that our Creator is the friend of sinners. For in every doctrine of grace, every promise of joy, every deed of love, every divine attraction presented in the Saviour's life on earth, we see 'God with us.' "[7]

Jesus, the Firstborn of all creation

QUESTION **3** How is Jesus described in Colossians 1:15–17?

> He is the image of the invisible God, the firstborn over all creation. For by Him all things were created that are in heaven and that are on earth, visible and invisible, whether thrones or dominions or principalities or powers. All things were created through Him and for Him. And He is before all things, and in Him all things consist (Colossians 1:15–17).

What does it mean that Jesus was the "firstborn" of all creation? "Firstborn" refers to one who has the privileges and prerogatives of God. Jesus is firstborn in the sense of privilege, *not* in the sense of time. All the privileges of the firstborn are His.

David was the eighth son of Jesse, yet called the firstborn (Psalm 89:27). Jesus declared that He was the "I AM," meaning the self-existent One: "before Abraham was, I AM" (John 8:58). The name "I AM" is the name God used to identify Himself to Moses (Exodus 3:14). Commenting on John 8, *The Desire of Ages* states, "The name of God, given to Moses to express the idea of the eternal presence, had been claimed as His own by this Galilean Rabbi. He had announced Himself to be the self-existent One, He who had been

promised to Israel, 'whose goings forth have been from of old, from the days of eternity' Micah 5:2."[8]

Isaiah the prophet calls Him the "everlasting Father" (see Isaiah 9:6). In calling Jesus the "Everlasting Father," Isaiah ties Jesus to the name *Jehovah*. Ellen White further explains the significance of this name: "Jehovah, the eternal, self-existent, *uncreated One*, Himself the Source and Sustainer of all, is alone entitled to supreme reverence and worship."[9] She also writes, "Jehovah is the name given to Christ. 'Behold, God is my salvation,' writes the prophet Isaiah; 'I will trust, and not be afraid; for the Lord JEHOVAH is my strength and my song; He also is become my salvation.' . . . 'Trust ye in the Lord forever; for in the Lord JEHOVAH is everlasting strength.' "[10]

Jesus truly is from everlasting to everlasting.

Jesus' relationship with the Father

QUESTION **4** How did Jesus describe His relationship with the Father?

> Jesus said to him, "Have I been with you so long, and yet you have not known Me, Philip? He who has seen Me has seen the Father; so how can you say, 'Show us the Father'?" (John 14:9).

From the days of eternity, the Lord Jesus Christ was one with the Father and was the image of God. John says,

> In the beginning was the Word, and the Word was with God, and the Word was God. He was in the beginning with God. All things were made through Him, and without Him nothing was made that was made. . . .
>
> And the Word became flesh and dwelt among us, and we beheld His glory, the glory as of the only begotten of the Father, full of grace and

18

truth (John 1:1–3, 14).

The following statements from Ellen White confirm the fact that Jesus Christ existed with the Father from all eternity. "Christ, the Word, the only begotten of God, was one with the eternal Father—one in nature, in character, in purpose—the only being that could enter into all the counsels and purposes of God."[11]

"From the days of eternity the Lord Jesus Christ was one with the Father; He was 'the image of God,' the image of His greatness and majesty, 'the outshining of His glory.' It was to manifest this glory that He came to our world."[12]

"From all eternity Christ was united with the Father, and when He took upon Himself human nature, He was still one with God."[13] "In speaking of His pre-existence, Christ carries the mind back through dateless ages. He assures us that there never was a time when He was not in close fellowship with the eternal God. He to whose voice the Jews were then listening had been with God as one brought up with Him."[14]

Jesus' character

QUESTION **5** What does John reveal Jesus' character is really like?

"As the Father loved Me, I also have loved you; abide in My love. . . .

"Greater love has no one than this, than to lay down one's life for his friends" (John 15:9, 13).

Jesus, provides us a picture of the Father's character, and the Bible declares that God—Father, Son, and Holy Spirit—is love (1 John 4:8). The very character of God is love. His law is love. "Love to man is the earthward manifestation of the love of God. It was to implant this love, to make us children of one family, that the King of glory became one with us. And when His parting words are fulfilled, 'Love one another, as I have loved you' (John 15:12); when we love the world as He has loved it, then for us His mission is accomplished. We are fitted for heaven; for we have heaven in our hearts."[15]

Jesus came to reveal what God is like. The Savior's life of sacrificial, unselfish ministry paints a picture of a God whose love for us can never be exhausted. The following statement summarizes the practical ways Jesus treated people:

Jesus did not suppress one word of truth, but He uttered it always in love. He exercised the greatest tact and thoughtful, kind attention in His relationships with the people. He was never rude, never needlessly spoke a severe word, never gave needless pain to a sensitive soul. He did not censure human weakness. . . . In all men He saw fallen souls whom it was His mission to save.

Such is the character of Christ as revealed in His life.[16]

19

Jesus was tenderhearted, loving, and kind to everyone He came in contact with—what an example for us! To be like Jesus is the longing of my heart!

Jesus, our Creator and Friend

QUESTION **6** What does the eternal, all-powerful, loving Christ call us?

"No longer do I call you servants, for a servant does not know what his master is doing; but I have called you friends" (John 15:15).

What a privilege! The Divine Son of God calls us His friends. His greatest joy will be to introduce us as His friends to His Father one day soon.

How wonderful that our Creator calls us His friends. Truly, He created us for Himself, "for by Him all things were created that are in heaven and that are on earth, visible and invisible, whether thrones or dominions or principalities or powers. All things were created through Him and for Him" (Colossians 1:16). Through Creation, Jesus has revealed His eternal, almighty power.

- ■ Jesus is eternal.
- ■ Jesus is all-powerful.
- ■ Jesus reflects the loving character of God.
- ■ Jesus is the Creator.
- ■ Jesus is our Friend.

Jesus is our best Friend. Being a friend of Jesus brings contentment, inner peace, and joy that the world does not know. Although we are social beings and our earthly friends provide us with much of life's joy, Jesus, our best Friend, provides us a depth of happiness beyond comparison. We never need to feel alone. We have a wonderful friend in Jesus.

The following statement from Ellen White is so encouraging: "Your only safety and happiness are in making Christ your constant counselor. You can be happy in Him if you had not another friend in the wide world. . . . Your heavenly Father means to teach you to find in Him the friendship and love and consolation that will satisfy your most earnest hopes and desires."[17]

I love the old song written in 1855 by John M. Scriven, "What a Friend We Have in Jesus." Each phrase speaks of the depth of Jesus' friendship.

What a friend we have in Jesus,
All our sins and griefs to bear;
What a privilege to carry
Everything to God in prayer!
O what peace we often forfeit,
O what needless pain we bear,
All because we do not carry
Everything to God in prayer.

Have we trials and temptations?
Is there trouble anywhere?
We should never be discouraged;
Take it to the Lord in prayer!
Can we find a friend so faithful,
Who will all our sorrows share?

Jesus knows our every weakness;
Take it to the Lord in prayer!

Are we weak and heavy laden,
Cumbered with a load of care?
Precious Savior, still our refuge,

Take it to the Lord in prayer.
Do thy friends despise, forsake thee?
Take it to the Lord in prayer!
In His arms He'll take and shield thee,
Thou wilt find a solace there.[18]

Jesus' greatest desire

QUESTION **7** What is Jesus Christ's greatest desire?

"And this is eternal life, that they may know You, the only true God, and Jesus Christ whom You have sent" (John 17:3).

_____

_____

As we meditate upon the life of Christ, we discover what God is really like. Jesus' great longing is for us to know the Father as He knows the Father and that we love His Father as He loves His Father.

Would you like to open your heart to a new or possibly renewed relationship with Jesus? Would you like to say, "Yes, Jesus, I believe You are the eternal, everlasting Christ, and I choose to be Your friend forever"? If so, check the box below:

☐ I choose to be Jesus' friend forever.

The next lesson will unfold the greatest drama in the universe, enabling us to more fully understand the great controversy between Christ and Satan—a titanic struggle between good and evil. The origin of sin and the reason for its existence is very perplexing to many people. In our next lesson, we will discover what is really behind the pain and suffering in the universe and what a loving God is doing about it.

Although it is not possible to explain the origin of sin and give a reason for its existence, we can still understand the justice and mercy of God in all His dealings with evil. The Scriptures plainly teach that God was in no way responsible for the entrance of sin. Sin is a mysterious intruder. But there is hope for this sinful world. Let's learn about it!

---

1. Ellen G. White, _Education_ (Mountain View, CA: Pacific Press®, 1952), 73.
2. Ellen G. White, _Selected Messages,_ book 1 (Washington, DC: Review and Herald®, 1958), 247.
3. Ellen G. White, _Patriarchs and Prophets_ (Nampa, ID: Pacific Press®, 2005), 36; emphasis added.
4. White, 38; emphasis added.
5. Ellen G. White, _Evangelism_ (Washington, DC: Review and Herald®, 1946), 615; emphasis added.
6. Ellen G. White, _The Desire of Ages_ (Nampa, ID: Pacific Press®, 2005), 19.
7. White, 24.
8. White, 469, 470.

9. White, *Patriarchs and Prophets*, 305; emphasis added.

10. Ellen G. White, "The Word Made Flesh," *Signs of the Times*, May 3, 1899, 2.

11. White, *Patriarchs and Prophets*, 34.

12. White, *Desire of Ages*, 19.

13. Ellen G. White, "Christ Our Only Hope," *Signs of the Times*, August 2, 1905, 10.

14. Ellen G. White, "Resistance to Light. No. 3," *Signs of the Times*, August 29, 1900, 3.

15. White, *Desire of Ages*, 641.

16. Ellen G. White, *Steps to Christ* (Washington, DC: Review and Herald®, 1977), 12.

17. Ellen G. White, *Our High Calling* (Washington, DC: Review and Herald®, 1961), 64.

18. Joseph M. Scriven, "What a Friend We Have in Jesus" (1855).

LESSON 2

Jesus and the Great Controversy

Have you ever wondered why there is so much pain in our world? *Why* do innocent people suffer? *Where* did evil come from? *Who* is responsible? Is there really a God who cares? The Bible *clearly answers* these questions. It reveals a titanic struggle in the universe termed by many as "the great controversy" between good and evil. It also unfolds God's final solution to the problem of sickness, suffering, and death.

The object of this lesson is to explore the great controversy between Christ and Satan, between truth and error. Our study will is to reveal the character of God and the designs of the devil. This lesson will reveal God's justice and love in dealing with the problem of evil. We will discover the central role of Christ in this cosmic conflict. The entire issue of the great controversy between Christ and Satan is really a battle over five issues:

- The *true character of God*—Is He really a God of unbounded, endless, unselfish love?
- The *unchangeable law of God*—Is the law really given for our good? Is it really unchangeable?
- The *true character of Satan*—Are his charges against God true?
- The *creative power of Christ*—Is Christ's creative power exclusively His? Why won't He share it with other beings in the universe?
- The *supremacy of Christ*—Why should Christ have the supremacy over Lucifer? Is God truly fair and just?

Jesus' true character

The first major issue in the great controversy between Christ and Satan focuses on the true character of God. The central theme of the great controversy between good and evil is God's unchanging love. Satan's strategy is to misrepresent the character of God. He wants the entire universe to regard God with fear rather than love. Satan's goal is that all of God's created beings have a false conception of the Creator.

This great controversy between Christ and Satan has been waged through the centuries. This lesson will establish and reveal God's true character. It will unfold life's greatest drama, enabling us to understand the great controversy more clearly. It will also uncover the reason why so many innocent people suffer.

We will see the true character of Satan in direct contrast to the unselfish, loving character of Christ.

The true character of Satan was revealed to the entire universe during Jesus' life and ministry on this earth. Satan's plot to destroy Jesus revealed the evil one as a liar and murderer. Although Satan saw Christ's love and mercy that revealed God's loving character, it only hardened him in rebellion. "It was Satan that prompted the world's rejection of Christ. The prince of evil exerted all his power and cunning to destroy Jesus; for he saw that

the Saviour's mercy and love, His compassion and pitying tenderness, were representing to the world the character of God."[1]

Jesus' death on the cross demonstrates His true character. It is the ultimate revelation of His love for humanity. God was willing to give His only begotten Son, the Creator of the universe, to die in our place. "For God so loved the world that He gave His only begotten Son, that whoever believes in Him should not perish but have everlasting life" (John 3:16).

QUESTION **1** What is the character of God like?

Beloved, let us love one another, for love is of God; and everyone who loves is born of God and knows God. He who does not love does not know God, for God is love. In this the love of God was manifested toward us, that God has sent His only begotten Son into the world, that we might live through Him. In this is love, not that we loved God, but that He loved us and sent His Son to be the propitiation for our sins. Beloved, if God so loved us, we also ought to love one another. . . .

. . . And we have known and believed the love that God has for us. God is love, and he who abides in love abides in God, and God in him (1 John 4:7–11, 16).

_____

_____

"God is love." The very character of God and His law is love. The law of love is the very foundation of the government of God. "God desires from all His creatures the service of love—service that springs from an appreciation of His character. He takes no pleasure in a forced obedience; and to all He grants freedom of will, that they may render Him voluntary service."[2] The prophet Jeremiah

gives us assurance about the character of God. "The LORD has appeared of old to me, saying, 'Yes, I have loved you with an everlasting love; therefore with lovingkindness I have drawn you' " (Jeremiah 31:3).

Throughout both the Old and New Testaments, God is revealed as a God of love who loves each one of us with an everlasting love beyond human comprehension.

26

QUESTION 2 How did Jesus reveal His love for the human race?

Let this mind be in you which was also in Christ Jesus, who, being in the form of God, did not consider it robbery to equal with God, but made Himself of no reputation, taking the form of a bondservant, and coming in the likeness of men. And being found in appearance as a man, He humbled Himself and became obedient to the point of death, even the death of the cross (Philippians 2:5–8).

For God so loved the world that He gave His only begotten Son, that whoever believes in Him should not perish but have everlasting life (John 3:16).

The death of Christ upon the cruel cross is a real demonstration of the love that God has for each one of us. God chose to pay the price of sin Himself by giving His only Son, Jesus Christ, to die for this world. The Cross reveals that the wages of sin is death. When Jesus cried out on the cross, "It is finished!" (John 19:30), Satan's doom was sealed. Christ's ultimate victory in the great controversy was then guaranteed. On the cross, God's justice, mercy, and love were manifested to the angels and the entire universe. Satan's true character was revealed. "In the contest between Christ and Satan, during the Saviour's earthly ministry, the character of the great deceiver was unmasked. Nothing could so effectually have uprooted Satan from the affections of the heavenly angels and the whole loyal universe as did his cruel warfare upon the world's Redeemer."[3]

The consequence of sin is death. Sin separates us from God, who is the source of all life. Once Adam and Eve sinned, they were under the curse of sin. Since the wages of sin is death, our first parents faced the death penalty.

But God had a plan. Jesus consented to give His life as a ransom to save humanity. However, the Father did not give up Christ easily. There was a struggle in the Father's heart. It was only because "God so loved the world that He gave His only begotten Son, that whoever believes in Him should not perish but have everlasting life" (John 3:16).

Ellen White's *Story of Redemption* makes this thought-provoking statement:

Said the angel, "Think ye that the Father yielded up His dearly beloved Son without a struggle? No, no. It was even a struggle with the God of heaven, whether to let guilty man perish, or to give His beloved Son to die for him." Angels were so interested for man's salvation that there could be found among them those who would yield their glory and give their life for perishing man, "But," said my accompanying angel, "that would avail nothing. The transgression was so great that an angel's life would not pay the debt. Nothing but the death and intercessions of His Son would pay the debt and save lost man from hopeless sorrow and misery."[4]

The cross was a painful experience for the Father. "The cross is a revelation to our dull senses of the pain that, from its very inception, sin has brought to the heart of God."[5]

The true portrait of Jesus is as the One with infinite love and supreme compassion. In no way can the pain and suffering in our world be attributed to God.

QUESTION 3   What is the true character of Satan, or the devil, like?

"You are of your father the devil, and the desires of your father you want to do. He was a murderer from the beginning, and does not stand in the truth, because there is no truth in him. When he speaks a lie, he speaks from his own resources, for he is a liar and the father of it" (John 8:44).

Jesus unmasks the character of Satan:

- He is a murderer from the beginning.
- He is a liar and the father of lies.

Satan declares that God is unfair and unjust. The evil one sowed disaffection throughout the heavenly realms. He declared that God was a selfish tyrant who desired love but would not give love in return.

Jesus' law is unchangeable

Since the law of God is a transcript of His loving character and the foundation of His government, it is unchangeable. If God's law could be changed, Adam would not have had to suffer the penalty of transgression. "The wages of sin is death" (Romans 6:23).

The central issue in the great controversy between Christ and Satan is over God's character, His law, government, and supremacy. Jesus' coming to this earth to redeem humanity revealed the character of God before the entire universe and His loving character in His law. It is unchangeable! It is immutable!

Jesus' death on the cross accomplishes five particularly important things in the battle between good and evil:

1. It reveals God's amazing love.
2. It provides eternal salvation for all those who would by faith accept Christ's sacrifice.
3. It demonstrates that God's law, the transcript of His character, is unchangeable.
4. It defeats death.
5. It guarantees Satan's ultimate destruction.

The cross proves that the very foundation of God's government is loving, just, and merciful. It is the eternal assurance of Christ's victory over death. It guarantees Satan's ultimate defeat. "Inasmuch then as the children have partaken of flesh and blood, He Himself likewise shared in the same, that through death He might destroy him who had the

power of death, that is, the devil" (Hebrews 2:14).

Ellen White adds this observation: "It was not merely to accomplish the redemption of man that Christ came to the earth to suffer and to die. He came to 'magnify the law' and to 'make it honorable.' Not alone that the inhabitants of this world might regard the law as it should be regarded; but it was to demonstrate to all the worlds of the universe that God's law is unchangeable. . . . The death of Christ proves it immutable."[6] It is impossible to change God's law. If the law could be changed, there would have been no reason for Jesus Christ to come to this world and endure all the ridicule, suffering, pain, and death. Truly, "if the law could be changed, man might have been saved without the sacrifice of Christ; but the fact that it was necessary for Christ to give His life for the fallen race, proves that the law of God will not release the sinner from its claims upon him. It is demonstrated that the wages of sin is death."[7]

Jesus' creative power

When we see the vast universe God has created, we realize how God is truly all-powerful. The power of God is absolutely amazing. Look at the clouds, the sky, the heavens, and all of nature, and you will be amazed at God's power. Psalm 62:11 says, "God has spoken once, twice I have heard this: that power belongs to God." Jesus is the Creator of all things. He laid the foundations of the earth (Psalm 104:5). Jesus is the Creator and the Life-Giver. He alone is worthy of our worship (Revelation 4:11).

Lucifer longed for Christ's creative power, desired the prerogatives of God, and wanted the supremacy of Christ. But he is a created being, and only the One who is life can give life.

Jesus' supremacy

Lucifer felt it was unfair for Jesus Christ to have supremacy over him. "The exaltation of the Son of God as equal with the Father was represented as an injustice to Lucifer, who, it was claimed, was also entitled to reverence and honor."[8] In addition, Satan "had sought to falsify the word of God and had misrepresented His plan of government, claiming that God was not just in imposing laws upon the angels; that in requiring submission and obedience from His creatures, He was seeking merely the exaltation of Himself. It was therefore necessary to demonstrate before the inhabitants of heaven, and of all the worlds, that God's government is just, His law perfect. . . . The true character of the usurper and his real object must be understood by all. He must have time to manifest himself by his wicked works."[9]

Jesus and the origin of evil

The Bible reveals the issues in the great controversy between Christ and Satan. Let's spend a few moments studying this amazing story. We learned in our last lesson that Jesus is the Lord of all things. He is the Creator of the entire universe. But if Jesus is the Creator of all things, did He create evil? Is He ultimately responsible for the heartache, pain, and suffering in our world?

The origin of evil and the reason for its existence greatly perplex many people. It is impossible to explain sin's origin and give a reason for its existence. However, the Bible reveals what goes on behind the scenes in the amazing celestial conflict, a battle between good and evil. The Scriptures plainly teach that God is in no way responsible for the evil in our world. "The entrance of sin into heaven cannot be explained. If it were explainable, it would show that there was some reason for sin. But as there was not the least excuse for it, its origin will ever remain shrouded in mystery."[10]

"God is love" (1 John 4:16). Love is the very foundation of God's government. If God's nature and His law are love, where did evil come from? Why was sin permitted? In this lesson, we will seek answers from the Bible.

It is impossible to explain the origin of sin so as to give a reason for its existence. Yet enough may be understood concerning both the origin and the final disposition of sin to make fully manifest the justice and benevolence of God in all His dealings with evil. Nothing is more plainly taught in Scripture than that God was in no wise responsible for the entrance of sin; that there was no arbitrary withdrawal of divine grace, no deficiency in the divine government, that gave occasion for the uprising of rebellion. Sin is an intruder, for whose presence no reason can be given. It is mysterious, unaccountable; to excuse it is to defend it. Could excuse for it be found, or cause be shown for its existence, it would cease to be sin.[11]

The Bible teaches that sin originated with Lucifer, one of God's created angels. Let's go back to the beginning of the controversy in heaven. God created tens of thousands of heavenly angelic beings. One of those angels God created was a being of dazzling brightness called Lucifer. The Bible says of Lucifer, "You were perfect in your ways from the day you were created, till iniquity was found in you" (Ezekiel 28:15).

God did not create an evil angel. God created Lucifer, a perfect angel, beautiful, noble, and upright. God exalted him to a position of high honor among the angelic host. However, God also created him with the power of choice. Lucifer abused his God-given power of choice. He rebelled against God, perverted his character, and became the devil. "He who sins is of the devil, for the devil has sinned from the beginning. For this purpose the Son of God was manifested, that He might destroy the works of the devil" (1 John 3:8).

God created all the angels full of goodness and love; it was their delight to do His will, and they loved God supremely. Perfect harmony existed throughout the universe. The law of love was the foundation of God's government. A question that many ask is, "What happened?" Although sin is a mystery and no complete reason can be found, we do get some good insights from Scripture. Speaking about Lucifer, Ezekiel declares,

"You were the seal of perfection,
Full of wisdom and perfect in beauty.
You were in Eden, the garden of God;
Every precious stone was your covering. . . .

"You were the anointed cherub who
   covers;
I established you;
You were on the holy mountain of God;
You walked back and forth in the midst of
   fiery stones.
You were perfect in your ways from the
   day you were created,
Till iniquity was found in you" (Ezekiel
   28:12–15).

When God created angels, He gave them the ability to choose. God did not want puppets to serve Him mindlessly. Genuine love necessitates a choice. But, in doing this, God took an awesome risk. These heavenly beings could choose to follow Him or rebel against Him. They could choose to love Him or walk away from His love.

Some people may ask, "Why did God create Lucifer with the power of choice? Why didn't God make Lucifer so that he automatically had to obey?" The answer is

simple. God did not want robot beings. He did not want a computer-chip angel that would respond every time God pushed a button. God did not want a robot or a computer, so He gave His angels intelligent minds with the power to choose. God wanted His creatures to serve Him out of love. Love cannot be programmed or forced; it must be voluntary.

God gave Lucifer the power of choice. Without the power of choice, God's creatures would not have the opportunity to really love. Without love, they would not have the opportunity to be fully happy.

Jesus responds to Lucifer's rebellion

QUESTION **4** Since God created Lucifer as a perfect angel, what caused him to rebel?

"How you are fallen from heaven,
O Lucifer, son of the morning!
How you are cut down to the ground,
You who weakened the nations!
For you have said in your heart:
'I will ascend into heaven,
I will exalt my throne above the stars of God;
I will also sit on the mount of the congregation
On the farthest sides of the north;
I will ascend above the heights of the clouds,
I will be like the Most High'" (Isaiah 14:12–14).

"Your heart was lifted up because of your beauty;
You corrupted your wisdom for the sake of your splendor;
I cast you to the ground,
I laid you before kings,
That they might gaze at you" (Ezekiel 28:17).

The Bible says in Ezekiel 28:17 that Lucifer's heart was lifted up because of his beauty. Pride dominated his life. Sin, evil, and death are the result of disobedience that originated with Satan. Self-centeredness was at the heart of Lucifer's rebellion. The book of Proverbs says, "Pride goes before destruction, and a haughty spirit before a fall" (Proverbs 16:18).

Lucifer said,

"*I* will ascend into heaven,
I will exalt my throne above the stars of God;
I will also sit on the mount of the congregation
On the farthest sides of the north;

I will ascend above the heights of the
    clouds,
I will be like the Most High" (Isaiah 14:13,
    14; emphasis added).

Why did Lucifer say, "I will ascend into heaven"? Wasn't he already in heaven? Yes, but Lucifer, a being of dazzling brightness, was, "not content with his position, though honored above the heavenly host, he [Lucifer] ventured to covet homage due alone to the Creator. Instead of seeking to make God supreme in the affections and allegiance of all created beings, it was his endeavor to secure their service and loyalty to himself. And coveting the glory with which the infinite Father had invested His Son, this prince of angels aspired to power that was the prerogative of Christ alone."[12]

The central issue in the controversy between good and evil was a battle for the throne. *Throne* implies a kingdom, law, and authority. Lucifer wanted to undermine God's government, His authority, and His laws. He wanted to rule from God's throne. He wanted to make laws and require obedience. "Pride in his own glory nourished the desire for supremacy. The high honors conferred upon Lucifer were not appreciated as the gift of God and called forth no gratitude to the Creator.

He gloried in his brightness and exaltation, and aspired to be equal with God."[13]

Lucifer had an "I" problem. "I" is the center of pride. Lucifer became proud, thinking his wisdom was his own rather than from God. He was dissatisfied with the position God had given him.

His disaffection was proved to be without cause, and he was made to see what would be the result of persisting in revolt. Lucifer was convinced that he was in the wrong. He saw that "the Lord is righteous in all His ways, and holy in all His works" (Psalm 145:17); that the divine statutes are just, and that he ought to acknowledge them as such before all heaven. Had he done this, he might have saved himself and many angels. He had not at that time fully cast off his allegiance to God. . . . He nearly reached the decision to return, but pride forbade him. It was too great a sacrifice for one who had been so highly honored to confess that he had been in error, that his imaginings were false, and to yield to the authority which he had been working to prove unjust.[14]

Jesus and the war in heaven

QUESTION **5**   What happened in heaven as a result of Satan's rebellion?

And war broke out in heaven: Michael and his angels fought with the dragon; and the dragon and his angels fought, but they did not prevail, nor was a place found for them in heaven any longer (Revelation 12:7, 8).

War in heaven! Lucifer's selfishness, greed, and pride resulted in war in heaven. That seems like such a strange place to have war, but, tragically, it happened. Now the destiny of the entire universe was at stake. For the first time, angels in heaven felt their affections being lured away from the Creator. Every angel had to decide whose side they were on. Every angel had to make a decision.

The reason we have war on earth is that there was first a war in heaven. Christ and His angels fought against the devil and his angels. Eventually, "the great dragon was cast out, that serpent of old, called the Devil and Satan, who deceives the whole world; he was cast to the earth, and his angels were cast out with him" (Revelation 12:9).

God dealt wisely with Satan's rebellion. He knew that,

The inhabitants of heaven and of other worlds, being unprepared to comprehend the nature or consequences of sin, could not then have seen the justice and mercy of God in the destruction of Satan. Had he been immediately blotted from existence, they would have served God from fear rather than from love. The influence of the deceiver would not have been fully destroyed, nor would the spirit of rebellion have been utterly eradicated. Evil must be permitted to come to maturity. For the good of the entire universe through ceaseless ages Satan must more fully develop his principles; that his charges against the divine government might be seen in their true light by all created beings, that the justice and mercy of God and the immutability of His law might forever be placed beyond all question.[15]

God was not unjust in casting Satan out of heaven. The Word of God is plain: "The LORD God, merciful and gracious, longsuffering, and abounding in goodness and truth, keeping mercy for thousands, forgiving iniquity and transgression and sin, by no means clearing the guilty" (Exodus 34:6, 7).

In great mercy, according to His divine character, God bore long with Lucifer. The spirit of discontent and disaffection had never before been known in heaven. It was a new element, strange, mysterious, unaccountable. Lucifer himself had not at first been acquainted with the real nature of his feelings; for a time he had feared to express the workings and imaginings of his mind; yet he did not dismiss them. He did not see whither he was drifting. . . . Though he had left his position as covering cherub, yet if he had been willing to return to God, acknowledging the Creator's wisdom, and satisfied to fill the place appointed him in God's great plan, he would have been reinstated in his office.[16]

Although Lucifer was convinced of his wrongdoing, he did not repent of his rebellion. He did not experience genuine sorrow for his sin. He was convinced about one thing: all he lost. He was not concerned about the pain he caused God's heart and the havoc he created in the universe. He wanted to be reinstated in heaven only to regain what he had lost. When he was fully convinced that he had gone too far and that there was no possibility of being reinstated to God's favor, he went forward with all malice and hatred. He would now try to gain control of God's new creation, planet Earth. He would try to destroy the happiness of our first parents, Adam and Eve. He would try to thrust them into rebellion, fully knowing this would cause untold grief in heaven.

In another lesson, we will study more fully how Satan deceived Adam and Eve, and we will also study the plan of redemption. But, what will be the outcome at the end of the great controversy?

Jesus wins; Satan loses!

Although the last chapter in this story of the great controversy between Jesus Christ and Satan has not yet been written, it can be summed up in four simple words: Jesus wins; Satan loses! Jesus has done something in the past to save all those who accept Him, His teachings, and His laws. He died to redeem us!

Jesus exalted as High Priest

Jesus is doing something now in the heavenly courts above. After Christ's ascension, He began His work as our High Priest. The Father has exalted Jesus as High Priest in the heavenly sanctuary. Since Jesus' death on the cross and His ascension, He has been interceding for us in the courts above. What is His work? "It was the work of the priest in the daily ministration to present before God the blood of the sin offering, also the incense which ascended with the prayers of Israel. So did Christ plead His blood before the Father in behalf of sinners, and present before Him also, with the precious fragrance of His own righteousness, the prayers of penitent believers. Such was the work of ministration in the first apartment of the sanctuary in heaven."[17]

QUESTION **6** Where is Jesus presently, and what is He doing for us?

Seeing then that we have a great High Priest who has passed through the heavens, Jesus the Son of God, let us hold fast our confession. For we do not have a High Priest who cannot sympathize with our weaknesses, but was in all points tempted as we are, yet without sin. Let us therefore come boldly to the throne of grace, that we may obtain mercy and find grace to help in time of need (Hebrews 4:14–16).

Therefore He is also able to save to the uttermost those who come to God through Him, since He always lives to make intercession for them.

For such a High Priest was fitting for us, who is holy, harmless, undefiled, separate from sinners, and has become higher than the heavens; who does not need daily, as those high priests, to offer up sacrifices, first for His own sins and then for the people's, for this He did once for all when He offered up Himself. For the law appoints as high priests men who have weakness, but the word of the oath, which came after the law, appoints the Son who has been perfected forever (Hebrews 7:25–28).

Now, Jesus, our High Priest, "has not entered the holy places made with hands, which are copies of the true, but into heaven itself, now to appear in the presence of God for us" (Hebrews 9:24). Jesus Christ's work as High Priest in the heavenly sanctuary is for us. His forgiveness, mercy, pardon, and power are for all of us. From heaven's sanctuary, Jesus sends light and truth to our minds through His Holy Spirit.

He encourages our hearts with the supreme thought that He loves us more than we can ever imagine and will do whatever it takes to save us. He pleads our case before the entire universe, declaring that through His death on the cross, by His grace, those who come to Him are forgiven, justified, and adopted as His children.

The intercession of Christ in man's behalf in the sanctuary above is as essential to the plan of salvation as was His death upon the cross. By His death He began that work which after His resurrection He ascended to complete in heaven. We must by faith enter within the veil, "whither the forerunner is for us entered." Hebrews 6:20. There the light from the cross of Calvary is reflected. There we may gain a clearer insight into the mysteries of redemption. The salvation of man is accomplished at an infinite expense to heaven; the sacrifice made is equal to the broadest demands of the broken law of God. Jesus has opened the way to the Father's throne, and through His mediation the sincere desire of all who come to Him in faith may be presented before God.[18]

By faith, we grasp the living reality that Jesus is our High Priest. He is interceding before the Father on our behalf. The Bible says there is only one thing that is impossible for God. The book of Hebrews tells us that *He cannot lie*. The promise is sure!

Thus God, determining to show more abundantly to the heirs of promise the immutability of His counsel, confirmed it by an oath, that by two immutable things, in which *it is impossible for God to lie*, we might have strong consolation, who have fled for refuge to lay hold of the hope set before us.

This hope we have as an anchor of the soul, both sure and steadfast, and which enters the Presence behind the veil, where the forerunner has entered for us, even Jesus, having become High Priest forever according to the order of Melchizedek (Hebrews 6:17–20; emphasis added).

Each of God's promises is true. Since it is impossible for God to lie, we can accept His Word as trustworthy. His Word declares that He has died for our sins. He is willing to forgive our sins and give us the power to live a new life, and He intercedes for us in the sanctuary above. He is coming again for us.

The question is often asked, Why doesn't Jesus do something about all the sin, suffering, and death in our world? He has, and all of His promises are ours to claim. We are a people of hope. The promise of His return will be fulfilled as His Word declares. Jesus Christ will come in the clouds of heaven with power and great glory one day soon! The entire universe will see the devastation Satan has brought upon the evil angels and this earth.

The ultimate fate of Satan is found in Ezekiel 28:19: "You have become a horror, and shall be no more forever." This is the final result of the great controversy—Satan is defeated and destroyed. In the end, he will be no more. The cross has proven that God is love.

The last chapter of the Bible's last book, Revelation, describes the conclusion of the "great controversy" in verses 3 and 4: "And there shall be no more curse, but the throne of God and of the Lamb shall be in it, and His servants shall serve Him. They shall see His face, and His name shall be on their foreheads."

When Christ cried out, "It is finished!" on the cross, He was pronouncing the death knell to sin and Satan. On the cross, Christ triumphed over the principalities and powers of hell. At the death of Christ, Satan's deadly grip on the human race was finished. His doom was sealed, and his ultimate fate assured. And one day, at the end of time, Satan will bear the responsibility for the sins he has enticed the entire human race to commit.

When the battle between Christ and Satan is finally over, it will be our glorious privilege to see Jesus face-to-face. It will be our greatest joy to live with Him through all eternity, where there is no sickness, pain, suffering, and death. "The great controversy is ended. Sin and sinners are no more. The entire universe is clean. One pulse of harmony and gladness beats through the vast creation. From Him who created all, flow life and light and gladness, throughout the realms of illimitable space. From the minutest atom to the greatest world, all things, animate and inanimate, in their unshadowed beauty and perfect joy, declare that God is love."[19]

On the one hand, Lucifer sought to be lifted up above Jesus Christ, but because of his pride and rebellion, he was cast down out of heaven.

On the other hand, Jesus humbled Himself and was exalted to the right hand of God in heaven. As a result of Christ's supreme sacrifice, what will the Father's response be? How will the entire universe react? "Therefore God also has highly exalted Him and given Him the name which is above every name, that at the name of Jesus every knee should bow, of those in heaven, and of those on earth, and of those under the earth" (Philippians 2:9, 10).

Now when He had taken the scroll, the four living creatures and the twenty-four elders fell down before the Lamb, each having a harp, and golden bowls full of incense, which are the prayers of the saints. And they sang a new song saying:

> "You are worthy to take the scroll,
> And to open its seals;
> For You were slain,
> And have redeemed us to God by Your blood
> Out of every tribe and tongue and people and nation,
> And have made us kings and priests to our God;
> And we shall reign on the earth"
> (Revelation 5:8–10).

If we would go up to heaven with Jesus, we must first come down to that "old rugged cross." I love the old song about Jesus giving His all on the cross. The message of salvation can be summed up in the inspiring song "The Old Rugged Cross."[20] Christ's victory on the cross settles the issues in the great controversy between good and evil forever. Let's spend a few moments contemplating the depth of the cross and the magnitude of His grace in the words of "The Old Rugged Cross":

> On a hill far away stood an old rugged cross,
> The emblem of suffering and shame,
> And I love that old cross where the dearest and best
> For a world of lost sinners was slain.
>
> So I'll cherish the old rugged cross,
> Till my trophies at last I lay down;
> I will cling to the old rugged cross,
> And exchange it someday for a crown.

Oh, that old rugged cross, so despised by
the world,
Has a wondrous attraction for me,
For the dear Lamb of God left His glory
above,
To bear it to dark Calvary.

To the old rugged cross, I will ever be true,
Its shame and reproach gladly bear;
Then He'll call me some day to my home
far away,
Where His glory forever I'll share.

One day all the inhabitants of the universe, both loyal and disloyal, will understand the righteousness and justice of God. They will understand that

"He is the Rock, His work is perfect;
For all His ways are justice,
A God of truth and without injustice;
Righteous and upright is He"
(Deuteronomy 32:4).

Would you like to say to Jesus today, "Yes, Jesus, I want to be on Your side, the winning side; I choose to stand with You against evil in earth's final controversy." If that is your desire, would you like to check the box below?

☐ In the great controversy between Christ and Satan, I want to be on Christ's side, the winning side.

In the next lesson, we will study about the creation of this world, the fall of our first parents, and the plan of redemption.

Although our first parents were created in the image of God, innocent and holy, they were not placed beyond the possibility of temptation. God made them free moral agents to choose obedience or disobedience. Before they could be eternally secure, their loyalty must be tested.

Let's learn more about it.

---

1. Ellen G. White, *The Great Controversy Between Christ and Satan* (Nampa, ID: Pacific Press®, 2005), 501.
2. Ellen G. White, *Patriarchs and Prophets* (Nampa, ID: Pacific Press®, 2005), 34.
3. White, *Great Controversy*, 501.
4. Ellen G. White, *The Story of Redemption* (Washington, DC: Review and Herald®, 1980), 45.
5. Ellen G. White, *Education* (Mountain View, CA: Pacific Press®, 1952), 263.
6. White, *Great Controversy*, 503.
7. White, *Patriarchs and Prophets*, 70.
8. White, 37.
9. White, 42.
10. Ellen G. White, "The Government of God," *Advent Review and Sabbath Herald*, March 9, 1886, 1.
11. White, *Great Controversy*, 492, 493.
12. White, *Patriarchs and Prophets*, 35.
13. White, *Great Controversy*, 495.
14. White, *Patriarchs and Prophets*, 39.
15. White, *Great Controversy*, 498, 499.
16. White, *Patriarchs and Prophets*, 39.
17. White, *Great Controversy*, 420, 421.
18. White, 489.
19. White, 678.
20. George Bennard, "The Old Rugged Cross" (1913).

NOTES

LESSON 3

Jesus, the Creator

The question in every lesson is, "Who is Jesus, and what difference does that make in my life?" Is He just a good man, another prophet, or the divine Son of God? When we understand who Jesus really is, our lives will be changed. We will appreciate Him more fully and worship Him more deeply.

Scripture presents many images of Christ. One of the most comprehensive is Colossians 1:15–20. It answers who Jesus is and the effect He has upon our lives. Colossians states that Jesus is the image of the invisible God (verse 15), the Creator (verse 16), the Sustainer of all living things (verse 17), the preeminent One (verse 18), the fullness of the Godhead (verse 19), and the Redeemer (verse 20). These eternal realities give Jesus the authority and power to redeem us through His blood, answer our prayers, deliver us from darkness, forgive our sins, adopt us into His family, and lead His church.

The early Christians were amazed as Paul unfolded who Jesus really is. When they understood Jesus' divinity, they were compelled to take the gospel (the good news) of Jesus Christ to the world. As we grasp who Jesus really is, we, too, will be motivated to share the good news with others around us.

Jesus Christ—the Creator

QUESTION **1** According to Colossians 1:15–17, who is the Creator of all things?

He is the image of the invisible God, the firstborn over all creation. For by Him all things were created that are in heaven and that are on earth, visible and invisible, whether thrones or dominions or principalities or powers. All things were created through Him and for Him. And He is before all things, and in Him all things consist (Colossians 1:15–17).

41

Jesus Christ is the Creator of the universe; He created the angels and all the other worlds (Hebrews 1:2). All created beings are dependent on life given by God. The Bible is plain. Jesus, created this world.

QUESTION **2** What biblical evidence is there that Jesus was an active Agent with God in Creation?

Then God said, "Let *Us* make man in *Our* image, according to *Our* likeness" (Genesis 1:26, emphasis added).

The words *Us* and *Our* are plurals, meaning more than one. God the Father, God the Son, and God the Holy Spirit all participated in Creation. The book of Hebrews confirms this. It clearly states that the worlds were made by *God's Son,* whom "He has appointed heir of all things, through whom also *He made the worlds*" (Hebrews 1:2).

Jesus, the active Agent in Creation

Jesus was the active Agent in Creation. Christ spread the heavens and laid the foundations of the whole earth. Jesus revealed Himself through His marvelous works of creation.

The entire universe rejoiced at the creation of planet Earth. Job 38:4, 7 says when "the foundations of the earth" were laid, "the morning stars sang together,

and all the sons of God shouted for joy." Hundreds of thousands of angelic beings sang songs of praise for the Creator at the time of earth's creation. The history of the world and the human race began as God created the heavens and the earth. Ephesians 3:9 says that He was given grace "to make all see what is the fellowship of the mystery, which from the beginning of the ages has been hidden in God who created all things through Jesus Christ" (Ephesians 3:9).

Let's go back to the beginning. "In the beginning God created the heavens and the earth" (Genesis 1:1). God is the Master Designer of the universe; Jesus carried out His Father's will in Creation through the power of the Holy Spirit. The earth that Father, Son, and Holy Spirit created was exceedingly beautiful. Can you imagine what the earth must have looked like when it came forth in all its Edenic splendor fresh from the hand of the Creator? Ellen White describes it this way:

> As the earth came forth from the hand of its Maker, it was exceedingly beautiful. Its surface was diversified with mountains, hills, and plains, interspersed with noble rivers and lovely lakes; but the hills and mountains were not abrupt and rugged, abounding in terrific steeps and frightful chasms, as they now do; the sharp, ragged edges of earth's rocky framework were buried beneath the fruitful soil, which everywhere produced a luxuriant growth of verdure. There were no loathsome swamps or barren deserts. Graceful shrubs and delicate flowers greeted the eye at every turn. The heights were crowned with trees more majestic than any that now exist. The air, untainted by foul miasma, was clear and healthful. The entire landscape outvied in

beauty the decorated grounds of the proudest palace. The angelic host viewed the scene with delight, and rejoiced at the wonderful works of God.[1]

Our wondering human minds ask the question, *How did God accomplish this?* The incredible reality is, God spoke, and the world came into existence. Jesus brought the heavens and the earth into existence by the power of His Word. David says, "By the word of the LORD the heavens were made, and all the host of them by the breath of His mouth" (Psalm 33:6). Truly, "the creative energy that called the worlds into existence is in the word of God. This word imparts power; it begets life. Every command is a promise; accepted by the will, received into the soul, it brings with it the life of the Infinite One. It transforms the nature and re-creates the soul in the image of God."[2]

At Creation, God's audible word was so powerful that it created something out of nothing; this is difficult for us to understand. Although Scripture clearly reveals many things about Creation, including the length of time it took to create planet Earth (Genesis 2:1, 2), it is not possible to know everything we would like to know. Commenting on Moses' explanation, Ellen White wrote, that " 'the secret things belong unto the Lord our God: but those things which are revealed belong unto us and to our children forever.' Deuteronomy 29:29. Just how God accomplished the work of creation He has never revealed to men; human science cannot search out the secrets of the Most High. His creative power is as incomprehensible as His existence."[3]

Jesus and the Creation week

A question that is often discussed is the length

of time it took to create this world. The Bible is extremely clear. Planet Earth was created in six days, and the Creator, Jesus, rested the seventh day from all His creative work. The Scriptures make this point plain.

QUESTION How can we be sure of the fact that Jesus created the world in a seven-day, literal week?

Then God saw everything that He had made, and indeed it was very good. So the evening and the morning were the sixth day.

Thus, the heavens and the earth, and all the host of them, were finished. And on the seventh day God ended His work which He had done, and He rested on the seventh day from all His work which He had done (Genesis 1:31–2:2).

A seven-day cycle is built into the very fabric of our being. The Creator not only left His fingerprint on everything He made but also left a seven-day biological cycle telling us that He made life in a seven-day Creation week.

Like the Sabbath, the week originated at creation, and it has been preserved and brought down to us through Bible history. God Himself measured off the first week as a sample for successive weeks to the close of time. Like every other, it consisted of seven literal days. Six days were employed in the work of creation; upon the seventh, God rested, and He then blessed this day, and set it apart as a day of rest for man. . . .

. . . The Bible recognizes no long ages in which the earth was slowly evolved from chaos. Of each successive day of creation, the sacred record declares that it consisted of the evening and the morning, like all other days that have followed.[4]

There is another perspective of the weekly cycle that is absolutely fascinating. Chronobiology is a relatively new science describing the interrelationship between time and the body's biological functions. There have been some fascinating findings regarding the weekly rhythms of the body, known as circaseptan rhythms—a seven-day cycle in which the biological processes of life, including disease symptoms and development, resolve.

Many of our body's biological rhythms actually function in seven-day cycles. Our energy is renewed in a seven-day cycle, and healing often occurs in a seven-day cycle. These medical facts about our body's seven-day rhythms are amazing. The God who created our body regulates its function.

The weekly cycle is not like the day, month, and year; it is not connected to astronomy. God established the week as a memorial of Creation. The same God who created our world preserves it.

It is not because of inherent power that year by year the earth produces her bounties and continues her motion around the sun. The hand of God guides the planets and keeps them in position in their orderly march through the heavens. . . .

God is the foundation of everything. All true science is in harmony with His works; all true education leads to obedience to His government. Science opens new wonders to our view; she soars high, and explores new depths; but she brings nothing from her research that conflicts with divine revelation. Ignorance may seek to support false views of God by appeals to science, but the book of nature and the written word shed light upon each other. We are thus led to adore the Creator and to have an intelligent trust in His word.[5]

It is interesting to note that each measurement of time has an astronomical basis except the week:

- The *year* is the time the earth takes to revolve around the sun.
- The *month* is the time the moon takes to orbit the earth.
- The *day* is the time the earth takes to make one full revolution on its axis.

Why is the seven-day weekly cycle so significant? At the conclusion of Creation week, the Bible says in Genesis, "And on the seventh day God ended His work which He had done, and He rested on the seventh day from all His work which He had done. Then God blessed the seventh day and sanctified it, because in it He rested from all His work which God had created and made" (Genesis 2:2, 3).

Jesus and the weekly cycle
In 1929–1940, the Russians gradually

introduced a five-day week. Although workers had a day off every week, there was not a particular day of rest. On September 1, 1931, the five-day week was replaced by a six-day week. They tried having a fixed day of rest, falling on the sixth, twelfth, eighteenth, twenty-fourth, and thirtieth day of each month. They had to use March 1 as the thirtieth day of February. After twelve years of failed production, weary workers, and a sagging economy, Stalin ordered a return to the seven-day weekly cycle.

During the French Revolution in the 1790s, the atheistic government of France altered the weekly cycle. This experiment in changing God's original plan also ended in dismal failure. Human beings were made to live in harmony with the Creator's natural laws.

He gave us six days to labor and the seventh day to rest. He is the Creator of the Sabbath; the seventh-day Sabbath is a day for healing. It provides an opportunity for restorative rest of mind and body. It is heaven's defense against unending work. By worshiping our Creator every Sabbath, our spiritual life is renewed. The cycle of life that the Creator has given us is written on every nerve and tissue of our body and cries out for renewal every seven days. Resting and worshiping on Sabbath places us in harmony with the laws of the universe.

Jesus and the creation of humanity
The Bible records the story of humanity's origin. We did not originate progressively from a single-celled amoeba or lower forms of life. We were created by an all-wise God, the Master Designer. The book of beginnings, Genesis, makes it plain that God created the humans in His own image. "So, God created man in His own image; in the image of God He created him; male and

female He created them" (Genesis 1:27).

God saw everything He made, and He was pleased with His work. It was very good. Believing the Scriptures just as they read leaves no ground for the supposition that humans evolved. This is detailed in the book *Patriarchs and Prophets*, by Ellen White:

"So, God created man in His own image; . . . male and female created He them." Here is clearly set forth the origin of the human race; and the divine record is so plainly stated that there is no occasion for erroneous conclusions. God created man in His own image. Here is no mystery. There is no ground for the supposition that man was evolved by slow degrees of development from the lower forms of animal or vegetable life. Such teaching lowers the great work of the Creator to the level of man's narrow, earthly conceptions. Men are so intent upon excluding God from the sovereignty of the universe that they degrade man and defraud him of the dignity of his origin. . . . The genealogy of our race, as given by inspiration, traces back its origin, not to a line of developing germs, mollusks, and quadrupeds, but to the great Creator. Though formed from the dust, Adam was "the son of God."[6]

Christ chose to make man in His own image. He spoke, and the entire world came into existence. But He fashioned Adam with His own hands: "And the LORD God formed man of the dust of the ground, and breathed into his nostrils the breath of life; and man became a living being" (Genesis 2:7).

In His infinite wisdom, God created man perfect. He was of great stature and perfect in symmetry. Adam was created in the image of God but was alone. He had no companion, no one to enter deep, intimate fellowship with. Then God caused Adam to sleep, and He removed a rib from Adam's sleeping form and made a woman. Eve reflected in her physical form and loving character the attributes of a loving God to meet Adam's deepest needs.

Adam and Eve complemented one another, each designed by an all-wise God to live for the other unselfishly. Their completeness was found in their relationship with each other and their relationship with their loving Creator. Describing our first parents, Ellen White tells us that Adam "was more than twice as tall as men now living upon the earth, and was well proportioned. His features were perfect and beautiful. . . . Eve was not quite as tall as Adam. Her head reached a little above his shoulders. She, too, was noble, perfect in symmetry, and very beautiful."[7]

A loving God created us. We did not evolve. The evolutionary theory leaves no room for an all-powerful God who spoke the world into existence by His creative Word. It denies the work of the Creator to create this world in six literal, continuous, twenty-four-hour days. It completely misses the point of the Sabbath as the everlasting memorial of Creation. Ellen White states it so clearly: "Many teach that matter possesses vital power—that certain properties are imparted to matter, and it is then left to act through its own inherent energy; and that the operations of nature are conducted in harmony with fixed laws, with which God Himself cannot interfere. This is false science, and is not sustained by the word of God."[8]

QUESTION **4** What was God's purpose in creating the earth?

For thus says the LORD,
Who created the heavens,
Who is God,
Who formed the earth and made it,
Who has established it,
Who did not create it in vain,
Who formed it to be inhabited:
"I am the LORD, and there is no other" (Isaiah 45:18).

God made the earth to be inhabited with happy, joyous people. He placed His children, Adam and Eve, in a beautiful Garden. This gorgeous Garden was to be their home. Beautifully colored flowers dotted the landscape. The birds sang their joyous songs. Best of all, their Creator, the God of the universe, regularly visited the Garden to fellowship with them.

Before sin, our first parents, Adam and Eve, fellowshiped with Jesus face-to-face. True happiness was found in communion with God. Adam and Eve experienced true joy as they worked in the Garden, enjoyed their natural surroundings, and communed with their Maker. He gave them the Sabbath. God set aside the Sabbath as an eternal memorial of His creative power. In a sinless world, happiness filled the hearts of Adam and Eve.

Jesus never intended for there to be any sadness. He never intended that humans experience sickness, suffering, or pain.

Jesus and the fall of humanity

God granted Adam and Eve freedom of choice. Their love, loyalty, and obedience to God could be fully revealed to the entire unfallen universe only if they were given the opportunity to choose obedience or disobedience. Adam and Eve were well aware of the fall of Lucifer. The tree of knowledge of good and evil was a test of their obedience to God. "And the LORD God commanded the man, saying, 'Of every tree of the garden you may freely eat; but of the tree of the knowledge of good and evil you shall not eat, for in the day that you eat of it you shall surely die' " (Genesis 2:16, 17). God created Adam and Eve with the capacity to choose. They were free moral agents. They could obey God and live, or they could disobey and die.

Satan "shuddered at the thought of plunging the holy, happy pair into the misery and remorse he was himself enduring. He seemed in a state of indecision: at one time firm and determined, then hesitating and wavering. His angels were seeking him, their leader, to acquaint him with their decision. They would unite with Satan in his plans, and with him bear the responsibility and share the consequences."[9] Finally, Satan grew determined to make Adam and Eve disobey God. Lucifer, the fallen angel, would attempt to destroy the happiness of the human pair.

No longer free to stir up rebellion in heaven, Satan's enmity against God found a new field in plotting the ruin of the human race. In the happiness and peace of the holy pair in Eden he beheld a vision of the bliss that to him was forever lost. Moved by envy, he determined to incite them to disobedience, and bring upon them the guilt and penalty of sin. He would change their love to distrust and their songs of praise to reproaches against their Maker. Thus he would not only plunge these innocent beings into the same misery which he was himself enduring, but would cast dishonor upon God, and cause grief in heaven.[10]

Eve's first mistake was wandering away from her husband. Eve gazed upon the forbidden tree with curiosity. Now was Satan's opportunity as he approached her through the serpent. The serpent was the most cunning of all the beasts of the earth. Eve paused when she heard the serpent speak: "And he said to the woman, 'Has God indeed said, "You shall not eat of every tree of the garden"?' " (Genesis 3:1).

Eve's second mistake was carrying on a conversation with the serpent. This was dangerous. Eve's conversation with the serpent was another step that led toward the path of being deceived. Satan came as a liar and deceiver. She did not initially recognize that the serpent was the fallen angel, Lucifer.

And the woman said to the serpent, "We may eat the fruit of the trees of the garden; but of the fruit of the tree which is in the midst of the garden, God has said, 'You shall not eat it, nor shall you touch it, lest you die.' "

Then the serpent said to the woman, "You will not surely die. For

48

God knows that in the day you eat of it your eyes will be opened, and you will be like God, knowing good and evil" (Genesis 3:2–5).

Eve's third mistake was believing the serpent and not obeying God's clear instructions. It must have been strange for Eve to hear a serpent contradict God. Step-by-step, she surrendered to the serpent's deception. Eve should have immediately fled and told Adam, but she didn't. She lingered and listened. Finally, the temptation was more than Eve could handle. She rushed headlong into sin. What a price was paid for dallying with Satan!

Eve's final mistake was seizing and eating the forbidden fruit. "So when the woman saw that the tree was good for food, that it was pleasant to the eyes, and a tree desirable to make one wise, she took of its fruit and ate. She also gave to her husband with her, and he ate" (Genesis 3:6). Eve reached her hand out and took the fruit. It seemed as if it wouldn't matter much if she touched the forbidden fruit. Then the temptation was more than she could stand. Eve took the fruit and ate it. She gathered more fruit and gave it to Adam and told him what had happened.

An expression of sadness came over the face of Adam. He appeared astonished and alarmed. To the words of Eve he replied that this must be the foe against whom they had been warned; and by the divine sentence she must die. In answer she urged him to eat, repeating the words of the serpent, that they should not surely die. She reasoned that this must be true, for she felt no evidence of God's displeasure, but on the contrary realized a delicious, exhilarating influence, thrilling every faculty with new life, such, she

imagined, as inspired the heavenly messengers.

Adam understood that his companion had transgressed the command of God, disregarded the only prohibition laid upon them as a test of their fidelity and love. There was a terrible struggle in his mind. He mourned that he had permitted Eve to wander from his side. But now the deed was done; he must be separated from her whose society had been his joy. How could he have it thus? Adam had enjoyed the companionship of God and of holy angels. He had looked upon the glory of the Creator. He understood the high destiny opened to the human race should they remain faithful to God. Yet all these blessings were lost sight of in the fear of losing that one gift which in his eyes outvalued every other. Love, gratitude, loyalty to the Creator—all were overborne by love to Eve. She was a part of himself, and he could not endure the thought of separation. He did not realize that the same Infinite Power who had from the dust of the earth created him, a living, beautiful form, and had in love given him a companion, could supply her place. He resolved to share her fate; if she must die, he would die with her.[11]

Jesus' promise

The tree of knowledge of good and evil was a test of love and obedience to God. If we love God, we will obey Him. It was a simple test—but a very important test. Obedience brings life. Disobedience brings death. The destiny of this entire planet was at stake in this test in Eden.

It was not God's desire for humanity to experience sin, suffering, or death. He wanted us to live eternally. The result of our first parents' sin meant death to Adam and Eve and all of humanity. "For the wages of sin is death, but the gift of God is eternal life in Christ Jesus our Lord" (Romans 6:23).

QUESTION 5 What promise did God give to our first parents when they sinned?

"And I will put enmity
Between you and the woman,
And between your seed and her Seed;
He shall bruise your head,
and you shall bruise His heel" (Genesis 3:15).

A bruise on the head is a deadly blow. A bruise on the heel, though painful, is not necessarily deadly. Jesus gave the death blow to Satan on the cross.

The question is often asked, Why doesn't God do something about all the suffering and death in our world? He has done something! He has not only created us but also redeemed us.

Commenting on Genesis 3:15, Ellen White wrote, "This sentence, uttered in the hearing of our first parents, was to them a promise. While it foretold war between man and Satan, it declared that the power of the great adversary would finally be broken. . . . Though they must suffer from the power of their mighty foe, they could look forward to final victory."[12]

QUESTION 6 Why was Adam and Eve's sin so serious?

Therefore, just as through one man sin entered the world, and death through sin, and thus death spread to all men, because all sinned—(For until the law sin was in the world, but sin is not imputed when there is no law. Nevertheless, death reigned from Adam to Moses, even over those who had not sinned according to the likeness of the transgression of Adam, who is a type of Him who was to come) (Romans 5:12–14).

The Bible records that Christ, the Second Adam, would face the devil head-on and redeem Adam's failure. Our Savior would face the evil one's temptations in common with all humanity. As Scripture says, He "was in all points tempted as we are, yet without sin" (Hebrews 4:15).

The difference between Jesus' temptations and Adam's was vast. Adam was tempted on one point in the innocence of Eden. Jesus was tempted on every point possible after the human race had deteriorated for more than four thousand years. Jesus also faced the full

brunt of Satan's temptations. Satan used all his hellish power to get Jesus to sin, but Satan failed. Jesus was victorious. Jesus' life of loving service and obedience unto death revealed the eternal nature of God's law. Ellen White writes, "I saw that it was impossible for God to change His law in order to save lost, perishing man; therefore He suffered His darling Son to die for man's transgressions."[13] Furthermore, she states,

> The law of God is as sacred as God Himself. It is a revelation of His will, a transcript of His character, the expression of divine love and wisdom. The harmony of creation depends upon the perfect conformity of all beings, of everything, animate and inanimate, to the law of the Creator. God has ordained laws for the government, not only of living beings, but of all the operations of nature. . . .
>
> Like the angels, the dwellers in Eden had been placed upon probation; their happy estate could be retained only on condition of fidelity to the Creator's law. They could obey and live, or disobey and perish.[14]

"Many who teach that the law of God is not binding upon man, urge that it is impossible for him to obey its precepts. But if this were true, why did Adam suffer the penalty of transgression? . . . The law of God can no more be transgressed with impunity now than when sentence was pronounced upon the father of mankind."[15]

The breaking of God's law demanded the life of the sinner. Adam and Eve recognized the result of their sin. They now saw death all around them in the drooping, dying flowers and falling leaves. At the sight of death, they wept bitterly. The fall of God's beloved children filled all heaven with sorrow. There appeared no escape for humanity, who had transgressed the law. Jesus' heart of love was moved with compassion for the lost world:

> The Son of God, heaven's glorious Commander, was touched with pity for the fallen race. His heart was moved with infinite compassion as the woes of the lost world rose up before Him. But divine love had conceived a plan whereby man might be redeemed. The broken law of God demanded the life of the sinner. In all the universe there was but one who could, in behalf of man, satisfy its claims. Since the divine law is as sacred as God Himself, only one equal with God could make atonement for its transgression. None but Christ could redeem fallen man from the curse of the law and bring him again into harmony with Heaven. Christ would take upon Himself the guilt and shame of sin—sin so offensive to a holy God that it must separate the Father and His Son. Christ would reach to the depths of misery to rescue the ruined race.[16]

Jesus had a plan for the human race to be restored to God again. He revealed His plan to all the angels of heaven. The angels did not rejoice as Christ opened to them the plan of redemption.

> The angels prostrated themselves at the feet of their Commander and offered to become a sacrifice for man. But an angel's life could not pay the debt; only He who created man had power to redeem him. Yet the angels were to have a part to act in the plan of redemption. . . .
>
> Christ assured the angels that by His death He would ransom many, and would destroy him who had the power of death. . . .
>
> Then joy, inexpressible joy, filled heaven. The glory and blessedness of a world redeemed, outmeasured even the anguish and sacrifice of the Prince of life. . . . With a deeper gladness now than in the rapture of the new creation, "the morning stars sang together, and all the sons of God shouted for joy." Job 38:7.
>
> To man the first intimation of redemption was communicated in the sentence pronounced upon Satan in the garden.[17]

QUESTION **7** Throughout the Bible, what are the two great acts of Jesus?

But now, thus says the LORD, who created you, O Jacob,
And He who formed you, O Israel:
"Fear not, for I have redeemed you;
I have called you by your name;
You are Mine" (Isaiah 43:1).

Christ's act of creating and His act of redeeming us assure us of His incalculable love. What a magnificent, awesome plan God has to restore us to Him. We will experience the wonders of His creative works more gloriously than at the beginning.

But in the final restitution, when there shall be "a new heaven and a new earth" (Revelation 21:1), it is to be restored more gloriously adorned than at the beginning.

Then they that have kept God's commandments shall breathe in immortal vigor beneath the tree of life; and through unending ages the inhabitants of sinless worlds shall behold, in that garden of delight, a sample of the perfect work of God's creation, untouched by the curse of sin—a sample of what the whole earth would have become, had man but fulfilled the Creator's glorious plan.[18]

Jesus is not only the Creator but also the Redeemer of the human race. In our next lesson, we will cover the plan of salvation. What is the plan? When was it established? How will the plan be carried out? What are the steps we can take to accept Jesus' plan? The next subject will be Jesus, the Redeemer.

Revelation declares,
"You are worthy, O Lord,
To receive glory and honor and power;
For You created all things,
And by Your will they exist and were
    created" (Revelation 4:11).

What a wonderful Christ we serve!

In your own spiritual life, how has Jesus revealed Himself as both your Creator and your Redeemer?

1. Ellen G. White, *Patriarchs and Prophets* (Nampa, ID: Pacific Press®, 2005), 44.

2. Ellen G. White, *Education* (Mountain View, CA: Pacific Press®, 1952), 126.

3. White, *Patriarchs and Prophets*, 113.

4. White, 111, 112.

5. White, 115, 116.

6. White, 44, 45.

7. Ellen G. White, *The Story of Redemption* (Washington, DC: Review and Herald®, 1980), 21.

8. White, *Patriarchs and Prophets*, 114.

9. White, *The Story of Redemption*, 28, 29.

10. White, *Patriarchs and Prophets*, 52.

11. White, 56.

12. White, 65, 66.

13. Ellen G. White, *Early Writings* (Washington, DC: Review and Herald®, 1945), 127.

14. White, *Patriarchs and Prophets*, 52, 53.

15. White, 61.

16. White, 63.

17. White, 64, 65.

18. White, 62.

NOTES

LESSON

Jesus, the Redeemer

The fall of Adam and Eve plunged the entire human race into a life of misery and death and filled all heaven with pain and sorrow. The beautiful world that God created was blighted with the curse of sin. Angels no longer sang their songs of praise. All of heaven mourned over the ruin of humanity. Jesus was filled with compassion for the fallen race. He could not bear to be separated from them forever. He put into action a plan to rescue this world from the curse of sin.

The result of our first parents' sin meant death for Adam and Eve and the entire human race—they must pay the penalty of sin, which is death (Romans 6:23). Humans could not save themselves, "Therefore, . . . through one man sin entered the world, and death through sin, and thus death spread to all men, because all sinned" (Romans 5:12).

God's love would not allow Him to destroy Adam and Eve. But God's justice demanded that sin be paid with the wages of death. Death is the natural result of sin. What would a loving God do? How could God save this world He loved? How could He be just and merciful at the same time? For, "it was impossible for God to change His law in order to save lost, perishing man; therefore He suffered His darling Son to die for man's transgressions."[1]

Jesus—the greatest manifestation of God's love

QUESTION **1** What is the greatest manifestation of God's love?

In this the love of God was manifested toward us, that God has sent His only begotten Son into the world, that we might live through Him. In this is love, not that we loved God, but that He loved us and sent His Son to be the propitiation for our sins (1 John 4:9, 10).

_____

_____

Some of the material in this lesson is taken from previously published Bible studies, articles, and presentations by the authors.

The plan of salvation was devised before Creation, so when Adam and Eve chose to believe Satan's lies, God put His plan into action. Writing of this, Ellen White comments,

I saw the lovely Jesus and beheld an expression of sympathy and sorrow upon His countenance. Soon I saw Him approach the exceeding bright light which enshrouded the Father. Said my accompanying angel, He is in close converse with His Father. The anxiety of the angels seemed to be intense while Jesus was communing with His Father. Three times He was shut in by the glorious light about the Father, and the third time He came out from the Father, His person could be seen. His countenance was calm, free from all perplexity and doubt, and shone with benevolence and loveliness, such as words cannot express.

He then made known to the angelic host that a way of escape had been made for lost man. He told them that He had been pleading with His Father, and had offered to give His life a ransom, to take the sentence of death upon Himself, that through Him man might find pardon; that through the merits of His blood, and obedience to the law of God, they could have the favor of God and be brought into the beautiful garden and eat of the fruit of the tree of life.[2]

This is amazing! In addition, "from the beginning, God and Christ knew of the apostasy of Satan, and of the fall of man through the deceptive power of the apostate. God did not ordain that sin should exist, but He foresaw its existence, and made provision to meet the terrible emergency. So great was His love for the world, that He covenanted to give His only-begotten Son."[3] Only Jesus could step in and provide a way of salvation for lost humanity.

The Son of God, heaven's glorious Commander, was touched with pity for the fallen race. His heart was moved with infinite compassion as the woes of the lost world rose up before Him. But divine love had conceived a plan whereby man might be redeemed. The broken law of God demanded the life of the sinner. In all the universe there was but one who could, in behalf of man, satisfy its claims. Since the divine law is as sacred as God Himself, only one equal with God could make atonement for its transgression. None but Christ could redeem fallen man from the curse of the law and bring him again into harmony with Heaven. Christ would take upon Himself the guilt and shame of sin—sin so offensive to a holy God that it must separate the Father and His Son. Christ would reach to the depths of misery to rescue the ruined race.[4]

The plan of salvation ensures that all who by faith accept His sacrifice and respond to His love will be saved. It also vindicates the character of God. Satan claimed God is unfair and unjust. Christ's death on the cross revealed to a waiting world and the watching universe the depth of God's love. It answered Satan's charges that God was an authoritarian tyrant demanding obedience and giving little in return. The plan of salvation had cosmic implications in the controversy between good and evil. Ellen White pulls aside the curtain in this celestial drama:

But the plan of redemption had a yet

broader and deeper purpose than the salvation of man. It was not for this alone that Christ came to the earth; it was not merely that the inhabitants of this little world might regard the law of God as it should be regarded; but it was to vindicate the character of God before the universe. To this result of His great sacrifice—its influence upon the intelligences of other worlds, as well as upon man—the Saviour looked forward when just before His crucifixion He said: "Now is the judgment of this world: now shall the prince of this world be cast out. And I, if I be lifted up from the earth, will draw all unto Me." John 12:31, 32. The act of Christ in dying for the salvation of man would not only make heaven accessible to men, but before all the universe it would justify God and His Son in their dealing with the rebellion of Satan. It would establish the perpetuity of the law of God and would reveal the nature and the results of sin.[5]

Jesus' assurance of His unchangeable law

QUESTION **2** What assurance does Jesus give that the law of God could never be changed?

"Do not think that I came to destroy the Law or the Prophets. I did not come to destroy but to fulfill. For assuredly, I say to you, till heaven and earth pass away, one jot or one tittle will by no means pass from the law till all is fulfilled" (Matthew 5:17, 18).

God's law is eternal. It is a transcript of His character, the foundation of His government, and the revelation of His will. Why would God allow His Son to go through the agony of Gethsemane, the beatings in Pilate's judgment hall, the torture of the cross, and the condemnation of sin's wrath if all He had to do was wave a celestial wand and change His law? The truth is that the law is eternal.

If the law could be changed, man might have been saved without the sacrifice of Christ; but the fact that it was necessary for Christ to give His life for the fallen race, proves that the law of God will not release the sinner from its claims upon him. It is demonstrated that the wages of sin is death. . . The very fact that Christ bore the penalty of man's transgression is a mighty argument to all created intelligences that the law is changeless; that God is righteous, merciful, and self-denying; and that infinite justice and mercy unite in the administration of His government.[6]

Jesus' plan in advance

The plan of salvation was laid before the creation of the world. God planned ahead of time for the redemption of Adam and Eve. The apostle John declares that Jesus is "the

Lamb slain from the foundation of the world" (Revelation 13:8).

The apostle Peter also confirms that Jesus planned for the terrible emergency ahead of time by pledging His own life as a ransom for sin. "You were not redeemed with corruptible things, like silver or gold, from your aimless conduct received by tradition from your fathers, but with the precious blood of Christ, as of a lamb without blemish and without spot. He indeed was foreordained before the foundation of the world, but was manifest in these last times for you" (1 Peter 1:18–20).

In lesson 3, we learned that Jesus is the all-powerful Creator of the universe. In this lesson, we are discovering Jesus' plan to redeem the human race.

The plan for our redemption was not an afterthought, a plan formulated after the fall of Adam. It was a revelation of "the mystery which hath been kept in silence through times eternal." Romans 16:25, R. V. It was an unfolding of the principles that from eternal ages have been the foundation of God's throne. From the beginning, God and Christ knew of the apostasy of Satan, and of the fall of man through the deceptive power of the apostate. God did not ordain that sin should exist, but He foresaw its existence, and made provision to meet the terrible emergency. So great was His love for the world, that He covenanted to give His only-begotten Son, "that whosoever believeth in Him should not perish, but have everlasting life." John 3:16.[7]

Heaven's divine plan to rescue humanity from the penalty of sin would involve an infinite sacrifice. Jesus, "being in the form of God, did not consider it robbery to be equal with God, but made Himself of no reputation, taking the form of a bondservant, and coming in the likeness of men. And being found in appearance as a man, He humbled Himself and became obedient to the point of death, even the death of the cross" (Philippians 2:5–8).

Jesus—the greatest evidence of God's love

QUESTION **3** What is the greatest evidence of God's love for the world?

"For God so loved the world that He gave His only begotten Son, that whoever believes in Him should not perish but have everlasting life" (John 3:16).

The Father consented to the death of His only Son, Jesus, because of His great love for mankind. It is difficult to understand the depths of Heaven's great love, but throughout all eternity, the redeemed will praise God for Heaven's unspeakable gift.

Praise and adoration were poured forth for the self-denial and sacrifice of Jesus; that He would consent to leave the bosom of His Father and choose a life of suffering and anguish and die an ignominious death to give life to others.

60

Said the angel, "Think ye that the Father yielded up His dearly beloved Son without a struggle? No, no. It was even a struggle with the God of heaven, whether to let guilty man perish, or to give His beloved Son to die for him."[8]

Lucifer's rebellion in heaven was over the issue of self-exaltation. He wanted to usurp Christ's position and ascend to Christ's throne. Contrary to the grasping attitude of Satan, Jesus was willing to surrender His throne, give up the glories of heaven, and descend into this snake pit of a world to redeem us. "But we see Jesus, who was made a little lower than the angels, for the suffering of death crowned with glory and honor, that He, by the grace of God, might taste death for everyone" (Hebrews 2:9). Truly, "by His life and His death, Christ has achieved even more than recovery from the ruin wrought through sin. It was Satan's purpose to bring about an eternal separation between God and man; but in Christ we become more closely united to God than if we had never fallen. In taking our nature, the Saviour has bound Himself to humanity by a tie that is never to be broken. Through the eternal ages He is linked with us."[9] Furthermore, "through Christ's redeeming work the government of God stands justified. The Omnipotent One is made known as the God of love. Satan's charges are refuted, and his character unveiled. Rebellion can never again arise. Sin can never again enter the universe. Through eternal ages all are secure from apostasy. By love's self-sacrifice, the inhabitants of earth and heaven are bound to their Creator in bonds of indissoluble union."[10]

Jesus dies the cruelest death

Jesus died the cruelest of all deaths to save lost humanity. Jesus experienced ridicule, abuse, betrayal, and the suffering of the cross for us. He experienced physical, mental, and spiritual

61

agony for us. There is nothing like this in the universe. The gospels describe what our loving Savior endured:

> Then the soldiers of the governor took Jesus into the Praetorium and gathered the whole garrison around Him. And they stripped Him and put a scarlet robe on Him. When they had twisted a crown of thorns, they put it on His head, and a reed in His right hand. And they bowed the knee before Him and mocked Him, saying, "Hail, King of the Jews!" Then they spat on Him, and took the reed and struck Him on the head. And when they had mocked Him, they took the robe off Him, put His own clothes on Him, and led Him away to be crucified (Matthew 27:27–31).

> They cried out again, "Crucify Him!"
> Then Pilate said to them, "Why, what evil has He done?"
> But they cried out all the more, "Crucify Him!"
> So, Pilate, wanting to gratify the crowd, released Barabbas to them; and he delivered Jesus, after he had scourged Him, to be crucified (Mark 15:13–15).

Who is this that suffers so much pain and agony? It is Jesus, the Son of the Living God. It is Jesus, the Creator of the universe. When Jesus hung on the cross, He experienced more than the pain of the nails in His hands and feet, and the crown of thorns on His head. It was more than the blood running down His face. It was much more than physical suffering. When Jesus hung on the cross, the darkness of sin enshrouded Him, hiding Him from the Father's face. That is why, as Jesus hung there alone and dying, He cried out, "My God, My God, why have You forsaken Me?" (Matthew 27:46).

Jesus chose to suffer the penalty for Adam and Eve's sin. To explain this to them they "were told that since the law of Jehovah is the foundation of His government in heaven as well as upon the earth, even the life of an angel could not be accepted as a sacrifice for its transgression. Not one of its precepts could be abrogated or changed to meet man in his fallen condition, but the Son of God, who had created man, could make an atonement for him. As Adam's transgression had brought wretchedness and death, so the sacrifice of Christ would bring life and immortality."[11]

Jesus includes angels in the plan of redemption

QUESTION **4** What part were the angels to have in the plan of redemption?

> But to which of the angels has He ever said:

> "Sit at My right hand,
> Till I make Your enemies Your footstool"?

> Are they not all ministering spirits sent forth to minister for those who will inherit salvation? (Hebrews 1:13, 14).

The angels are to minister to us but also were to strengthen and minister to Jesus in His sufferings. "When the angels should witness the agony and humiliation of their Lord, they would be filled with grief and indignation and would wish to deliver Him from His murderers; but they were not to interpose in order prevent anything which they should behold. It was a part of the plan of redemption that Christ should suffer the scorn and abuse of wicked men, and He consented to all this when He became the Redeemer of man."[12]

QUESTION 5   What would man recover as a result of Jesus' sacrifice?

"And you, O tower of the flock,
The stronghold of the daughter of Zion,
To you shall it come,
Even the former dominion shall come,
The kingdom of the daughter of Jerusalem" (Micah 4:8).

By Jesus' sacrifice, not only would humans be redeemed, but they also would gain dominion once again over that which had been forfeited by sin. "Christ has redeemed us from the curse of the law, having become a curse for us (for it is written, 'Cursed is everyone who hangs on a tree')" (Galatians 3:13).

In the plan of salvation, Jesus bears the guilt of our sins. He credits His perfect righteousness to our account. We owe a sin debt that is impossible for us to pay. Jesus paid the debt by shedding His own precious blood. "Christ was treated as we deserve, that we might be treated as He deserves. He was condemned for our sins, in which He had no share, that we might be justified by His righteousness, in which we had no share. He suffered the death which was ours, that we might receive the life which was His. 'With His stripes we are healed.' "[13]

God's original purpose in creating man was to have holy, happy beings. This original purpose of God will be fulfilled by the redeemed of the earth. Christ's sacrifice enables the righteous—those who choose to follow Him—to one day again live in a beautiful world. "The righteous shall inherit the land, and dwell in it forever" (Psalm 37:29).

Jesus destroys death

QUESTION 6   How was Jesus to destroy the power of death and the devil forever?

Inasmuch then as the children have partaken of flesh and blood, He Himself likewise shared in the same, that through death He might destroy him who had the power of death, that is, the devil, and release those who through fear of death were all their lifetime subject to bondage (Hebrews 2:14, 15).

The angels were heartbroken at the thought of their Commander paying the price on behalf of lost humanity. But "Christ assured the angels that by His death He would ransom many, and would destroy him who had the power of death. . . . Sin and sinners would be blotted out, nevermore to disturb the peace of heaven or earth. He bade the angelic host to be in accord with the plan that His Father had accepted, and rejoice that, through His death, fallen man could be reconciled to God."[14]

Christ's death on the cross was the cruelest act in human history, the Just dying for the unjust, the Righteous dying for the unrighteous, the Innocent dying for the guilty. When Jesus cried, "It is finished," a shout of joy and triumph rang throughout heaven. The inhabited universe grasped that His sacrifice struck a death knell to Satan. They knew that Christ had conquered Satan. "The great contest that had been so long in progress in this world was now decided, and Christ was conqueror. His death had answered the question whether the Father and the Son had sufficient love for man to exercise self-denial and a spirit of sacrifice. . . . With one voice the loyal universe united in extolling the divine administration."[15]

Redemption comes through the cross of Calvary. Christ has taken the initiative in our salvation. He reached out to us before we reached out to Him. He seeks us before we seek Him. Jesus' death on the cross provides salvation for all humanity. Our role is to respond to His saving grace, by faith accepting what He has already done for us. The Bible says, "Believe on the Lord Jesus Christ, and you will be saved, you and your household" (Acts 16:31).

How can we be secure in the redemption that Jesus paid for on the cross of Calvary? The plan of salvation is very simple. There are five basic steps in the plan of salvation.

Step 1: Acknowledge (Psalm 51:3; Romans 3:23). First, we acknowledge that we have

sinned and need a Savior. Acknowledging our lost condition opens our hearts to receive everything Christ has for us. Failure to recognize our lostness without Christ prevents us from receiving His gift of salvation. It is only as we recognize our spiritual poverty that we will sense our need for the richness of His grace.

Step 2: Believe (John 3:16). The most often quoted text in the Bible states this truth clearly. "For God so loved the world that He gave His only begotten Son, that whoever believes in Him should not perish but have everlasting life. For God did not send His Son into the world to condemn the world, but that the world through Him might be saved" (John 3:16, 17). Ellen White adds,

> The heart of God yearns over His earthly children with a love stronger than death. In giving up His Son, He has poured out to us all heaven in one gift. The Saviour's life and death and intercession, the ministry of angels, the pleading of the Spirit, the Father working above and through all, the unceasing interest of heavenly beings,—all are enlisted in behalf of man's redemption.
>
> Oh, let us contemplate the amazing sacrifice that has been made for us![16]

You are so important to God that there is nothing that He would not do to save you. He has poured out all of heaven in Christ for your redemption and mine. There is nothing more He could do. Heaven has provided its most costly gift.

Step 3: Confess (1 John 1:9). Third, we confess our sins. Confession is our acknowledgment that we have failed and need a Savior; it is the recognition that we cannot save ourselves and are in desperate need of Christ's forgiveness. However, we have a

wonderful promise. "We should not try to lessen our guilt by excusing sin. We must accept God's estimate of sin, and that is heavy indeed. Calvary alone can reveal the terrible enormity of sin. If we had to bear our own guilt, it would crush us. But the sinless One has taken our place; though undeserving, He has borne our iniquity. 'If we confess our sins,' God 'is faithful and just to forgive us our sins and to cleanse us from all unrighteousness.' 1 John 1:9. Glorious truth!"[17]

Step 4: Repent (Acts 3:19). Fourth, we not only confess our sins but also repent of anything that the Holy Spirit impresses us with that is not in harmony with God's will.

How can we be just with God again? What shall we do to be saved? Salvation is only through Jesus Christ. We must repent of our sins and turn away from them. Repentance implies a change of attitude toward sin. We sense that our rebellion and sinful acts broke God's heart and choose to turn away from them forever. Peter called his listeners to "repent therefore and be converted, that your sins may be blotted out, so that times of refreshing may come from the presence of the Lord" (Acts 3:19). David wrote,

> Blessed is he whose transgression is
>   forgiven,
> Whose sin is covered.
> Blessed is the man to whom the LORD
>   does not impute iniquity,
> And in whose spirit there is no deceit
>   (Psalm 32:1, 2).

Also writing on repentance, Ellen White explains,

> But must the sinner wait till he has repented before he can come to Jesus? Is repentance to be made an obstacle between the sinner and the Saviour?

The Bible does not teach that the sinner must repent before he can heed the invitation of Christ, "Come unto Me, all ye that labor and are heavy-laden, and I will give you rest." Matthew 11:28. It is the virtue that goes forth from Christ, that leads to genuine repentance. . . . We can no more repent without the Spirit of Christ to awaken the conscience than we can be pardoned without Christ.[18]

Repentance is obtained only through Christ. It is beyond our power. We cannot accomplish it on our own. As we come to Christ just as we are, He imparts to us the gift of repentance. Jesus promises to give us the victory. Philippians 4:13 says, "I can do all things through Christ who strengthens me."

Step 5: Receive Him by faith (Revelation 3:20). Fifth, we not only acknowledge, believe, confess, and repent but also receive Him in our hearts by faith. The gospel of John states, "But as many as received Him, to them He gave the right to become the children of God, to those who believe in His name" (John 1:12). Faith is trusting His Word, accepting His promises, and believing what He has said is true. When we by faith receive Christ according to His Word, we become children of God, and as sons and daughters of God, we are heirs of eternal life. We believe it not because we feel it but because He declares it to be so.

The world's redeemer accepts men as they are, with all their wants, imperfections, and weaknesses; and He will not only cleanse from sin and grant redemption through His blood, but will satisfy the heart-longing of all who consent to wear His yoke, to bear His burden. It is His purpose to impart peace and rest to all who

come to Him for the bread of life. . . .

Through the right exercise of the will, an entire change may be made in your life. By yielding up your will to Christ, you ally yourself with the power that is above all principalities and powers. You will have strength from above to hold you steadfast, and thus through constant surrender to God, you will be enabled to live the new life, even the life of faith.[19]

Jesus enables humans to become children of God

QUESTION **7** What would the fallen children of God become as the result of Jesus' great sacrifice?

Beloved, now we are children of God; and it has not yet been revealed what we shall be, but we know that when He is revealed, we shall be like Him, for we shall see Him as He is (1 John 3:2).

_____

_____

Because of Christ's death on the cross, we have the privilege of becoming the children of God. "Through the cross we learn that the heavenly Father loves us with a love that is infinite. Can we wonder that Paul exclaimed, 'God forbid that I should glory, save in the cross of our Lord Jesus Christ'? Galatians 6:14. It is our privilege also to glory in the cross, our privilege to give ourselves wholly to Him who gave Himself for us. Then, with the light that streams from Calvary shining in our faces, we may go forth to reveal this light to those in darkness."[20] This is the most wonderful and exciting news in the world! His great sacrifice is incomprehensible, but by faith, I accept it:

☐ I accept His great sacrifice on the cross and desire to have a closer relationship with Him.

In the next lesson, we will discover more about Jesus' infinite sacrifice in coming to earth. Understanding His miraculous birth, we can more fully appreciate everything He has done for us. You will be thrilled as we study prophecies foretold hundreds of years in advance that testify to Christ as the Messiah.

1. Ellen G. White, *Early Writings* (Hagerstown, MD: Review and Herald®, 2000), 127.
2. Ellen G. White, *The Story of Redemption* (Washington, DC: Review and Herald®, 1980), 42.
3. Ellen G. White, *The Desire of Ages* (Nampa, ID: Pacific Press®, 2005), 22.
4. Ellen G. White, *Patriarchs and Prophets*, (Nampa, ID: Pacific Press®, 2005), 63.
5. White, 68, 69.
6. White, 70.
7. White, *Desire of Ages*, 22.
8. White, *Story of Redemption*, 44, 45.
9. White, *Desire of Ages*, 25.
10. White, 26.

11. White, *Patriarchs and Prophets*, 66, 67.

12. White, 65.

13. White, *Desire of Ages*, 25.

14. White, *Patriarchs and Prophets*, 65.

15. White, 70.

16. Ellen G. White, *Steps to Christ* (Washington, DC: Review and Herald®, 1977), 21.

17. Ellen G. White, *Thoughts From the Mount of Blessing* (Mountain View, CA, Pacific Press®, 1956), 116.

18. White, *Steps to Christ*, 26.

19. White, 46–48.

20. Ellen G. White, *The Acts of the Apostles* (Nampa, ID: Pacific Press®, 2005), 210.

NOTES

LESSON 5

Jesus, the Messiah of Prophecy

Have you ever wondered, *Is Jesus more than a good man, more than simply a moral teacher or philosopher? Who is Jesus? Is He really divine? Is He all He claimed to be?* What we believe about Jesus makes all the difference. If He is the divine Son of God, His offer of eternal life is true. If He is divine, He could transform our lives. In this lesson, we will study the indisputable evidence from the prophecies of the Old Testament and their fulfillment in the New Testament that Jesus is truly the world's Messiah.

The New Testament records a divine timetable for the birth of Jesus. "But when the fullness of the time had come, God sent forth His Son, born of a woman, born under the law" (Galatians 4:4). Expanding on this theme, Ellen White wrote, "The fullness of the time had come. Humanity, becoming more degraded through ages of transgression, called for the coming of the Redeemer. Satan had been working to make the gulf deep and impassable between earth and heaven. By his falsehoods he had emboldened men in sin. It was his purpose to wear out the forbearance of God, and to extinguish His love for man, so that He would abandon the world to satanic jurisdiction."[1]

Christ was born at precisely the right moment of human history. Violence, greed, and immorality had reached epidemic proportions. People were weary of pagan ideologies that left them fearful and afraid of the afterlife. They were tired of the powerless pageantry and traditions of Judaism. Roman roads united the civilized world. A common language was spoken throughout the empire. Minds were open. Hearts were receptive, and the Messiah was born.

Jesus came in God's perfect time

In Romans 5:6, the apostle Paul also discusses the divine timetable in Christ's life by declaring, "For when we were still without strength, in due time Christ died for the ungodly."

In some translations, the Greek word translated "due time" is instead translated "at the right time." Throughout biblical history, God has had a divine timetable of events. At exactly the right time, God sent His Son into the world to provide salvation for the human race. "Like the stars in the vast circuit of their appointed path, God's purposes know no haste and no delay. . . . So in heaven's council the hour for the coming of Christ had been determined. When the great clock of time pointed to that hour, Jesus was born in Bethlehem."[2]

Of the billions of babies born into this world, Jesus was unique. There was never a birth like His before, and there will never be a birth like His again. In this lesson, we will explore why Jesus' birth makes such a difference. We will discover amazing truths about our salvation and victory over temptation.

It was certainly a miraculous event that Jesus was born of Mary, a virgin. Both Matthew (Matthew 1:18–23) and Luke (Luke 1:30–38) declare that Jesus was born of a virgin. Although Joseph was engaged to Mary at the time of the announcement of Jesus' birth, Jesus is not simply the son of Joseph. Jesus is the Son of God.

Mary was the "highly favored" one because she would bear the Christ child. "Then the angel said to her, 'Do not be afraid, Mary, for you have found favor with God' " (Luke 1:30). She had "found favor with God," literally meaning she was "endowed with grace."

Later, the angel declared to Joseph, "She will bring forth a Son, and you shall call His name Jesus" (Matthew 1:21). The name *Jesus* means "Jehovah is salvation." Isaiah, the gospel prophet, made this thrilling prediction about the coming of the Messiah:

> For unto us a Child is born,
> Unto us a Son is given;
> And the government will be upon His
> shoulder.
> And His name will be called Wonderful,
> Counselor, Mighty God,
> Everlasting Father, Prince of Peace (Isaiah 9:6).

As the prophet states, "unto us a Son is given." Jesus left heaven for us. It was for us that He revealed the character of the Father. It was so we could behold His love that He touched blind eyes, unstopped deaf ears, healed withered bodies, and raised the dead. His life, death, and resurrection were for us.

At the birth of Jesus, Satan knew that One had come with a divine commission to dispute his dominion. He trembled at the angel's message attesting the authority of the newborn King. Satan well knew the position that Christ had held in heaven as the Beloved of the Father. That the Son of God should come to this earth as a man filled him with amazement and with apprehension. He could not fathom the mystery of this great sacrifice. . . . Since he had lost heaven, he was determined to find revenge by causing others to share his fall. This he would do by causing them to undervalue heavenly things, and to set the heart upon things of earth.[3]

Jesus' arrival brings joy to some shepherds

The shepherds were afraid when the angel appeared to them, but they were excited about the coming of the promised Savior. The shepherds discussed the promised Savior and prayed for the coming of the King, and it was to them that God sent angels to tell about the birth of the Savior.

> Above the hills of Bethlehem are gathered an innumerable throng of angels. They wait the signal to declare the glad news to the world. Had the leaders in Israel been true to their trust, they might have shared the joy of heralding the birth of Jesus. But now they are passed by. . . .
> . . . To those who are seeking for light, and who accept it with gladness, the bright rays from the throne of God will shine.[4]

How important it is for us to accept light and truth with gladness!

QUESTION **1** What sign did the angel give to the shepherds to prepare them to recognize their Savior?

"For there is born to you this day in the city of David a Savior, who is Christ the Lord. And this will be the sign to you: You will find a Babe wrapped in swaddling cloths, lying in a manger" (Luke 2:11, 12).

The angel's announcement stirred the shepherds' excitement. Ellen White describes the scene:

At these words, visions of glory fill the minds of the listening shepherds. The Deliverer has come to Israel! Power, exaltation, triumph, are associated with His coming. But the angel must prepare them to recognize their Saviour in poverty and humiliation. "This shall be a sign unto you," he says; "Ye shall find the babe wrapped in swaddling clothes, lying in a manger."

The heavenly messenger had quieted their fears. He had told them how to find Jesus. With tender regard for their human weakness, he had given them time to become accustomed to the divine radiance. Then the joy and glory could no longer be hidden. The whole plain was lighted up with the bright shining of the hosts of God. Earth was hushed, and heaven stooped to listen to the song,—

"Glory to God in the highest,
And on earth peace, good will toward men."

Oh that today the human family could recognize that song! The declaration then made, the note then struck, will swell to the close of time, and resound to the ends of the earth.[5]

QUESTION **2** What was the shepherds' response after they saw Baby Jesus?

Now when they had seen Him, they made widely known the saying which was told them concerning this Child. And all those who heard it marveled at those things which were told them by the shepherds. But Mary kept all these things and pondered them in her heart. Then the shepherds returned, glorifying and praising God for all the things that they had heard and seen, as it was told them (Luke 2:17–20).

The shepherd's hearts were filled with joy. They couldn't wait to share their experience that starry night of hearing the angel's song and seeing their dazzling brightness radiating in the sky. They were thrilled to tell their friends and neighbors how they were directed by the angels to find the Messiah. It is amazing that God would choose common shepherds to announce the birth of the Messiah. God loves to take common men and women, reveal the majesty of His grace to them, and send them out to tell the story of His love.

Jesus receives wise men from the East

QUESTION **3** Why were the wise men from the East so anxious to find the newborn King?

Now after Jesus was born in Bethlehem of Judea in the days of Herod the king, behold, wise men from the East came to Jerusalem, saying, "Where is He who has been born King of the Jews? For we have seen His star in the East and have come to worship Him" (Matthew 2:1, 2).

The wise men studied the prophecies of the Messiah, and they wanted to find and worship the newborn King. They followed the star that was predicted in Numbers 24:17, "A Star shall come out of Jacob, a Scepter shall rise out of Israel." *The Desire of Ages* tells us more about this wondrous star.

The magi learned with joy that His coming was near, and that the whole world was to be filled with a knowledge of the glory of the Lord.

The wise men had seen a mysterious light in the heavens upon that night when the glory of God flooded the hills of Bethlehem. As the light faded, a luminous star appeared, and lingered in the sky. It was not a fixed star nor a planet, and the phenomenon excited the keenest interest. That star was a distant company of shining angels, but of this the wise men were ignorant. Yet they were impressed that the star was of special import to them.[6]

Matthew 2:11 records the gifts the wise men gave to Baby Jesus. "And when they had come into the house, they saw the young Child with Mary His mother, and fell down and worshiped Him. And when they had opened their treasures, they presented gifts to Him: gold, frankincense, and myrrh" (Matthew 2:11). The visit from the wise men was a special picture of Jesus' larger mission to reach every human on earth.

The magi had been among the first to welcome the Redeemer. Their gift was the first that was laid at His feet. And through that gift, what privilege of ministry was theirs! The offering from the heart that loves, God delights to honor, giving it highest efficiency in service for Him. If we have given our

hearts to Jesus, we also shall bring our gifts to Him. Our gold and silver, our most precious earthly possessions, our highest mental and spiritual endowments, will be freely devoted to Him who loved us and gave Himself for us.[7]

These three gifts represented the totality of their lives—the gold represented all of their material possessions, frankincense was used in the worship service of the sanctuary, and myrrh was a healing balm. In these gifts, the wise men gave to Jesus all of their material possessions, their worship, and themselves. When we come to Jesus, we can never give Him just a part of ourselves; He only accepts wholehearted surrender.

Jesus' birth in Bethlehem prophesied

Seven hundred years before the birth of Christ, the prophet Micah predicted the exact birthplace of the Messiah. Of all the towns in Israel, the prophet, Micah, declares,

> "But you, Bethlehem Ephrathah,
> Though you are little among the thousands
>   of Judah,
> Yet out of you shall come forth to Me
> The One to be Ruler in Israel" (Micah 5:2).

The Gospel of Luke 2:4–7 confirms the fulfillment of this centuries-old prediction, "Joseph also went up from Galilee, out of the city of Nazareth, into Judea, to the city of David, which is called Bethlehem, because he was of the house and lineage of David, to be registered with Mary, his betrothed wife, who was with child. . . . And she brought forth her firstborn Son, and wrapped Him in swaddling cloths, and laid Him in a manger, because there was no room for them in the inn." This is a remarkable fulfillment of prophecy! Jesus was to be born in Bethlehem, and a decree of Caesar Augustus brought Mary and Joseph to Bethlehem just in time for Christ's birth. A Roman ruler unwittingly fulfilled Bible prophecy.

Notice this was not *any* Bethlehem, this was specifically Bethlehem Ephrathah in Judaea. There were two Bethlehems in Israel: one in the Galilee and the other in Judaea. Micah specifically predicted the Bethlehem in Judaea. Fulfilled prophecy testifies to Christ's divinity and the Bible's accuracy.

Jesus fulfills prophecy

The first prophecy of the coming of the Messiah is found in Genesis. God gave Adam and Eve this promise in Genesis 3:15.

> "And I will put enmity
> Between you and the woman,
> And between your seed and her Seed;
> He shall bruise your head,
> And you shall bruise His heel."

The word *enmity* means "opposed to" or "hostile to." When Adam and Eve sinned, they sided with Satan, but God promised to place a hostility in their hearts to the enticements and temptations of the enemy. By faith, they could look forward to the coming of the Messiah. Satan bruised Jesus on the cross, but in the very act of dying, Jesus gave the devil a deadly blow to his head.

There in the Garden of Eden, after our first parents sinned, God gave them a prophecy of hope. Adam and Eve must have wondered when the Messiah would appear. How long would they have to wait? Would He come in their lifetime? Adam and Eve eagerly looked forward to the day the Savior would appear. "The gospel was first preached to Adam by Christ. Adam and Eve felt sincere sorrow and repentance for their guilt. They believed the precious promise of God, and were saved from utter ruin."[8]

Bible prophecy describes the birth of Jesus in Isaiah 7:14—"Therefore the Lord Himself will give you a sign: Behold, the virgin shall conceive and bear a Son, and shall call His name Immanuel." The fulfillment of Isaiah 7:14 is found in Matthew 1:21—"And she will bring forth a Son, and you shall call His name *Jesus*, for He will save His people from their sins" (emphasis added). Jesus is the Savior. In truth,

heaven and earth are no wider apart today than when shepherds listened to the angels' song. . . .

The story of Bethlehem is an exhaustless theme. In it is hidden "the depth of the riches both of the wisdom and knowledge of God." Romans 11:33. We marvel at the Saviour's sacrifice in exchanging the throne of heaven for the manger, and the companionship of adoring angels for the beasts of the stall. Human pride and self-sufficiency stand rebuked in His presence. Yet this was but the beginning of His wonderful condescension.[9]

The fulfillment of Hosea 11:1 is found in Matthew 2:13. "When Israel was a child, I loved him, and out of Egypt I called My son" (Hosea 11:1). Matthew confirms Hosea's prediction: "Now when they had departed, behold, an angel of the Lord appeared to Joseph in a dream, saying, 'Arise, take the young Child and His mother, flee to Egypt, and stay there until I bring you word; for Herod will seek the young Child to destroy Him' " (Matthew 2:13).

It is absolutely amazing that Bible prophecy is so precise. Hosea, written thousands of years before the birth of the Christ Child, wrote that Jesus and His parents would flee to Egypt so Herod would not destroy Him.

The book of Revelation describes the satanic desire exemplified by Herod in his attempt to destroy Jesus as soon as He was born: "And the dragon stood before the woman who was ready to give birth, to devour her Child as soon as it was born" (Revelation 12:4). God miraculously protected His Son from the cunning plans of wicked men. As predicted, God provided a secure refuge for Jesus in Egypt.

Jesus' nature when He came to earth

QUESTION **4** What nature did Jesus take when he came to earth?

Inasmuch then as the children have partaken of flesh and blood, He Himself likewise shared in the same, that through death He might destroy him who had the power of death, that is, the devil, and release those who through fear of death were all their lifetime subject to bondage. For indeed He does not give aid to angels, but He does give aid to the seed of Abraham. Therefore, in all things He had to be made like His brethren, that He might be a merciful and faithful High Priest in things pertaining to God, to make propitiation for the sins of the people. For in that He Himself has suffered, being tempted, He is able to aid those who are tempted (Hebrews 2:14–18).

QUESTION **5** Why was it necessary for Jesus to take upon His divine nature our human nature?

Inasmuch then as the children have partaken of flesh and blood, He Himself likewise shared in the same, that through death He might destroy him who had the power of death, that is, the devil (Hebrews 2:14).

Therefore, in all things He had to be made like His brethren, that He might be a merciful and faithful High Priest in things pertaining to God, to make propitiation for the sins of the people (verse 17).

Jesus had to take our nature to be our Redeemer. Only One who faced the temptations of Satan in common with all humanity and overcame could qualify as our Savior. He could not be our perfect Example in overcoming sin and our dying Savior if He had an advantage over us. His life and His death reveal His likeness to each one of us. The Son of God became the Son of Man so that we could become sons and daughters of God.

It would have been an almost infinite humiliation for the Son of God to take man's nature, even when Adam stood in his innocence in Eden. But Jesus accepted humanity when the race had been weakened by four thousand years of sin. Like every child of Adam He accepted the results of the working of the great law of heredity. What these results were is shown in the history of His earthly ancestors. He came with such a heredity to share our sorrows and temptations, and to give us the example of a sinless life.[10]

Jesus' purpose in coming to Bethlehem's manger

QUESTION **6** Why did Jesus even come to earth?

"For the Son of Man has come to seek and to save that which was lost" (Luke 19:10).

_____

_____

Jesus came to earth to save the lost. Often Jesus referred to Himself as the Son of man. Throughout the New Testament, Jesus is revealed as the Son of God and the Son of man. Is Jesus fully God? Yes! Is Jesus fully man? Yes! With His divine arm, He reached up to heaven, and with His human arm, He reaches down to earth. Jesus is the bridge between the holy God and sinful man. Jesus came to earth after thousands of years of sin to enter the stream of time with the weaknesses of humanity. He came to share in our sorrows and all our temptations to give us an example of a sinless life.

Jesus' early life and childhood

QUESTION **7** What does the Bible indicate about Jesus' early life and childhood?

And the Child grew and became strong in spirit, filled with wisdom; and the grace of God was upon Him (Luke 2:40).

And Jesus increased in wisdom and stature, and in favor with God and men (verse 52).

Jesus is our ultimate example. "Since He gained knowledge as we may do, His intimate acquaintance with the Scriptures shows how diligently His early years were given to the study of God's word. And spread out before Him was the great library of God's created works. He who had made all things studied the lessons which His own hand had written in earth and sea and sky. . . . From His earliest years He was possessed of one purpose; He lived to bless others."[11] As we fill our minds with the Word of God and contemplate the things of eternity, we will be transformed into His image. There is life-changing power in the Word of God. Jesus filled His mind with the Scriptures, and we can too.

Jesus overcame temptation by the Word of God. He knew the Scriptures and responded with, "It is written." Often, Jesus' "young companions urged Him to do as they did. He was bright and cheerful; they enjoyed His presence, and welcomed His ready suggestions; but they were impatient at His scruples, and pronounced Him narrow and strait-laced. Jesus answered, It is written, 'Wherewithal shall a young man cleanse his way? by taking heed thereto according to Thy word.' 'Thy word have I hid in mine heart, that I might not sin against thee.' Psalm 119:9, 11."[12] However, "these adversaries of Christ had no arguments with which to meet the truths He brought home to their consciences. They could only cite their customs and traditions, and these seemed weak and vapid when compared with the arguments Jesus had drawn from the word of God and the unceasing round of nature."[13]

QUESTION **8** How do Jesus' temptations compare to our own?

For we do not have a High Priest who cannot sympathize with our weaknesses, but was in all points tempted as we are, yet without sin (Hebrews 4:15).

Satan tempted Jesus on every point possible with all possible power. Satan studies our weaknesses and tempts us on the points where he knows we are most vulnerable. Satan tempted Jesus on all points. Satan also unleashed all the power of each of these temptations on Jesus. There was nothing more he could tempt Jesus on and no more power he could bring forth. He tried everything, and it failed. Jesus overcame, and His power is available to us to overcome as well.

Temptation is not sin. Jesus was holy and pure; yet He was tempted in all points as we are, but with a strength and power that man will never be called upon to endure. In His successful resistance He has left us a bright example, that we should follow His steps. If we are self-confident or self-righteous we shall be left to fall under the power of temptation; but if we look to Jesus and trust in Him we call to our aid a power that has conquered the foe on the field of battle, and with every temptation He will make a way of escape.[14]

QUESTION 9 What lessons can we learn from Jesus' experience in the temple at age twelve?

Now so it was that after three days they found Him in the temple, sitting in the midst of the teachers, both listening to them and asking them questions. And all who heard Him were astonished at His understanding and answers. So when they saw Him, they were amazed; and His mother said to Him, "Son, why have You done this to us? Look, Your father and I have sought You anxiously."

And He said to them, "Why did you seek Me? Did you not know that I must be about My Father's business?" (Luke 2:46–49).

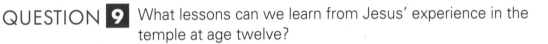

There is not a lot of information in the Bible about Christ's early childhood experiences. Some have called these the "silent years," but here is what we know for sure. Each time Christ's childhood is mentioned, He is "growing in wisdom and stature" with His mind saturated with Scripture. In the temple, He displays a superior knowledge and understanding of God's Word than the supposed learned priests. Jesus' childhood life is an example for all children and youth today. Every young person today has the opportunity to gain knowledge as Jesus did.

Jesus also had respect and love for His parents and was obedient to them. He was kind, tenderhearted, sympathetic, and compassionate to everyone. Jesus hated evil, and with every temptation, He turned away. He was eager to learn, so He increased in knowledge and wisdom.

As a twelve-year-old, Jesus began to understand the significance of His mission. The Holy Spirit gradually revealed to Him the purpose of His life. Jesus' question "Did you not know that I must be about My Father's business?" (Luke 2:49) summarizes His entire

life. His parents were caught up with the crowds at the Passover services in Jerusalem. They became so busy visiting with their friends and dealing with the ordinary duties of life that they did not realize that Jesus was missing. The book *The Desire of Ages* describes the reaction of His parents when they found Him after three days teaching in the temple:

> If Joseph and Mary had stayed their minds upon God by meditation and prayer, they would have realized the sacredness of their trust, and would not have lost sight of Jesus. By one day's neglect they lost the Saviour; but it cost them three days of anxious search to find Him. So, with us, by idle talk, evilspeaking, or neglect of prayer, we may in one day lose the Saviour's presence, and it may take many days of sorrowful search to find Him, and regain the peace that we have lost.[15]

The business of life today can often cause us to neglect our times of prayer and Bible study, and we, too, can lose the Savior's presence. Oh, how tragic that would be since Jesus gave so much for us. It is my heart's desire to worship the King of the universe always. If this is your desire, too, check the following box:

☐ I believe that Jesus is the true Messiah and accept Him as both my Savior and Lord. I choose to praise Jesus daily and give Him my whole life.

In the next lesson, we will share Jesus' example in baptism and the infilling of the Holy Spirit. His lifework was to accomplish the salvation of humanity. From His birth to His death, He had one goal: our redemption. From His resurrection to His return, He has one goal: our redemption. If we are that important to Jesus and our salvation is the object of His entire life, isn't it worth it to praise Him like the shepherds and give our whole life to Him like the wise men?

1. Ellen G. White, *The Desire of Ages* (Nampa, ID: Pacific Press®, 2005), 34, 35.

2. White, 32.

3. White, 115, 116.

4. White, 47.

5. White, 47, 48.

6. White, 60.

7. White, 65.

8. Ellen G. White, "Christ and the Law," *Advent Review and Herald of the Sabbath*, April 29, 1875, 138.

9. White, *Desire of Ages*, 48, 49.

10. White, 48, 49.

11. White, 70.

12. White, 89.

13. White, 208.

14. Ellen G. White, *Testimonies for the Church*, vol. 5 (Mountain View, CA: Pacific Press®, 1948), 426.

15. White, *Desire of Ages*, 83.

NOTES

LESSON 6

Jesus' Baptism and the Holy Spirit

Three of the four Gospels, Matthew, Mark, and Luke, tell the story of Christ's baptism. In each of these narratives, a heavenly anointing accompanies the baptism. At His baptism, Jesus received the Holy Spirit, and a voice from heaven declared, "This is my beloved Son, in whom I am well pleased" (see Matthew 3:16, 17; Mark 1:9–11; Luke 3:21, 22). These two divine realities reveal deep spiritual lessons to us as we study Christ's baptism.

In this lesson, we will discover important principles about Jesus' baptism that apply to our lives today. Jesus' baptism has lasting significance for our own spiritual growth. When Jesus was baptized, the Holy Spirit descended upon Him, giving Him strength for the temptations He would face. As we study Jesus' baptism, let's consider the following questions:

- What does Jesus' baptism say to us today?
- What does Jesus' baptism teach us about our own spiritual lives?
- How can we daily walk in the promise of the Holy Spirit's presence?
- Why is God's announcement, "This is

My beloved Son, in whom I am well pleased," so significant?

This event is filled with practical lessons. We begin by studying the life of John the Baptist as he prepared the way for the ministry of Jesus.

Jesus and John the Baptist

When John the Baptist was asked by the priests and Levites who he was, he answered them by saying:

"I am not the Christ."
    And they asked him, "What then? Are you Elijah?"
    He said, "I am not."
    "Are you the Prophet?"
    And he answered, "No."
    Then they said to him, "Who are you, that we may give an answer to those who sent us? What do you say about yourself?"
    He said: "I am

'The voice of one crying in the wilderness:
"Make straight the way of the LORD" ' "
        (John 1:20–23).

John's special ministry was to prepare the way for the coming of the Messiah. Through his preaching, hearts were touched and lives were changed. Men and women repented of their sins, were baptized, and lived a new life. Many of Jesus' followers were first the disciples of John.

God prepared the world for the coming of His Son through a divinely appointed messenger. Throughout Scripture, there is a providential pattern: God prepares the way for significant world events by sending a messenger with a message.

- Noah prepared the world for the Flood.
- Joseph prepared Egypt for the coming seven years of famine during the seven years of plenty.
- The prophets of Israel prepared the nation for coming destruction with messages of warning, calling them to repentance.

This divine pattern encapsulated in the ministry of John will be repeated in the last days of earth's history. Once again, God will have an urgent message to prepare the world for His second coming. Notice the following statement in *The Story of Redemption*: "John came in the spirit and power of Elijah to proclaim the first advent of Jesus. I was pointed down to the last days and saw that John represented those who should go forth in the spirit and power of Elijah to herald the day of wrath and the second advent of Jesus."[1]

As we study John's ministry of preparation, remember that it is a prelude to the last-day ministry of God's people to make ready a people for Christ's return. It is interesting to note that the priests and Levites were not as concerned about John's identity as they were about his authority to preach and teach. We see an example of this in their question. "And they asked him, saying, 'Why then do you baptize if you are not the Christ, nor Elijah, nor the Prophet?' " (verse 25).

QUESTION 1 What was John's response when he was asked who he was?

"Why then do you baptize if you are not the Christ, nor Elijah, nor the Prophet?"
John answered them, saying, "I baptize with water, but there stands One among you whom you do not know. It is He who, coming after me, is preferred before me, whose sandal strap I am not worthy to loose" (John 1:25–27).

The Scripture that John referred to is the prophecy of Isaiah 40:3.

The voice of one crying in the wilderness:
"Prepare the way of the LORD;
Make straight in the desert
A highway for our God."

Expanding on this calling, Ellen White writes, "When the Baptist began his ministry, many thought that he might be the prophet Moses risen from the dead, for he seemed to have a thorough knowledge of the prophecies and of the history of Israel."[2]

John's ministry was based on the authority of the prophetic Word. He was raised up by

God for a specific task at a specific time. The authority of God's last-day people to prepare the world for His return is also based on the prophetic Word.

QUESTION **2** How was John the Baptist to prepare the way for Jesus?

In those days John the Baptist came preaching in the wilderness of Judea, and saying, "Repent, for the kingdom of heaven is at hand!" For this is he who was spoken of the by the prophet Isaiah, saying:

"The voice of one crying in the wilderness:
'Prepare the way of the LORD;
Make His paths straight' " (Matthew 3:1–3).

For many Jews in the first century, religion became an endless round of ceremonies. They were locked in the ritualistic formality. John the Baptist's message spoke directly to their hearts, leading them to repentance. His words regarding the One to come opened their hearts and minds to receive the "good news" of the coming Messiah.

John the Baptist was the forerunner of Jesus. "John was to go forth as Jehovah's messenger to bring to men the light of God. He must give a new direction to their thoughts. He must impress them with the holiness of God's requirements, and their need of His perfect righteousness."[3]

QUESTION **3** What was John's reaction when he saw Jesus coming toward him?

The next day John saw Jesus coming toward him, and said, "Behold! The Lamb of God who takes away the sin of the world! This is He of whom I said, 'After me comes a Man who is preferred before me, for He was before me' " (John 1:29, 30).

John was the first to address Jesus as "the Lamb of God." John's statement reminds us of the ancient sanctuary. When sinners brought their sacrifice to the sanctuary, they were bowed down with guilt and laden with shame. They were condemned by the commandment they transgressed.

At the sanctuary, they confessed their sins over the head of the spotless lamb. The guilt, condemnation, and shame of sin were transferred from the sinner to the lamb. They must then take the knife and slay the lamb.

This entire sacrificial service was designed to teach the sinner that the only way to get rid of guilt was through the dying lamb. The sacrificial system revealed to Israel that there was a way for sin to be separated from the sinner. Though Israel's sins were symbolically placed on the lambs, one day, the sins of the world would be carried by the Messiah. Speaking prophetically of Jesus, Isaiah declared, "The LORD has laid on Him [Jesus] the iniquity of us all" (Isaiah 53:6).

The second great object lesson in the sanctuary is that sin causes pain. "Without shedding of blood there is no remission"

(Hebrews 9:22). Coming to Jesus, our dying Lamb, we confess our sins, and seeing the pain sin has caused Him, we choose to turn away from it forever. He is the Lamb that, through His sacrifice and by His blood, "takes away," or "bears away," the sin of the world, just as the Old Testament sacrificial system foretold. "By the figure of a lamb John identifies the suffering Messiah as the one in whom the sacrificial system of OT [Old Testament] times reaches reality and has meaning. In the divine foreknowledge and purpose, He was 'the Lamb slain from the foundation of the world.' (Rev. 13:8)."[4]

QUESTION 4 What was John's response to his questioners when asked whether he was the Christ?

John answered, saying to all, "I indeed baptize you with water; but One mightier than I is coming, whose sandal strap I am not worthy to loose. He will baptize you with the Holy Spirit and with fire" (Luke 3:16).

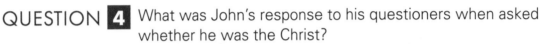

Although John baptized with water, Jesus would baptize with the Holy Spirit *and* fire. Notice the text does not say that Jesus would baptize with the Holy Spirit *or* with fire. What does this mean? The Greek New Testament word for baptism is *baptizō*. It means to fully immerse. It was used to describe a piece of cloth completely submerged in dye or a pot fully submerged in water to be filled. Fire in the Bible is always a symbol of the presence of God. Israel was led by a Pillar of fire in their wilderness wanderings. The fiery presence of God was manifest in the Shekinah glory in

the sanctuary. Elijah called down fire from heaven to consume the sacrifice on Mount Carmel. Divine fire repeatedly is equated with the divine presence. To be baptized with the Holy Spirit *and* fire means to be immersed in the presence of God. Jesus revealed God's presence on earth. To be intimately acquainted with Jesus through prayer and Bible study is to be baptized with the Holy Spirit. To be filled with the Spirit is to be filled with the Word, for Jesus said, "The words that I speak to you are spirit, and they are life" (John 6:63).

QUESTION **5** What act did John perform for people who had a new conversion?

"I indeed baptize you with water unto repentance, but He who is coming after me is mightier than I, whose sandals I am not worthy to carry. He will baptize you with the Holy Spirit and fire" (Matthew 3:11).

In baptizing people, "John proclaimed the coming of the Messiah, and called the people to repentance. As a symbol of cleansing from sin, he baptized them in the waters of the Jordan. Thus by a significant object lesson he declared that those who claimed to be the chosen people of God were defiled by sin, and that without purification of heart and life they could have no part in the Messiah's kingdom."[5]

Jesus set an example for us at the beginning of His ministry by being baptized. Matthew 3:13–15 says,

Then Jesus came from Galilee to John at the Jordan to be baptized by him. And John tried to prevent Him, saying, "I have need to be baptized by You, and are You coming to me?"

But Jesus answered and said to him, "Permit it to be so now, for thus it is fitting for us to fulfill all righteousness."

John felt unworthy to baptize the divine Son of God. When we are in the presence of Divinity, we, too, feel unworthy. When the light of Christ's holiness shines upon our sinfulness, we, too, respond with John, "Why are You coming to me?" One of the deeper lessons of Christ's baptism is that the Savior draws near to fallen humanity.

Jesus' example in baptism

QUESTION **6** How was Jesus baptized?

It came to pass in those days that Jesus came from Nazareth of Galilee, and was baptized by John in the Jordan. And immediately, coming up from the water, He saw the heavens parting and the Spirit descending upon Him like a dove. Then a voice came from heaven, "You are My beloved Son, in whom I am well pleased" (Mark 1:9, 10).

Jesus came up out of the water, indicating that John baptized by immersion. Baptism in the New Testament is full immersion because our natures are entirely fallen. The cleansing grace of Christ, symbolized by the waters of baptism, must saturate every part of our being. Baptism by immersion represents the death, burial, and resurrection of Christ. The person being baptized is completely covered by the water and rises from the water into a new life.

QUESTION **7** Why was it necessary for Jesus to be baptized?

But Jesus answered and said to him, "Permit it to be so now, for thus it is fitting for us to fulfill all righteousness." Then he allowed Him (Matthew 3:15).

Ellen White asserts, "Jesus did not receive baptism as a confession of guilt on His own account. He identified Himself with sinners, taking the steps that we are to take, and doing the work that we must do. His life of suffering and patient endurance after His baptism was also an example to us."[6] Jesus was not baptized because He had sinned. He was baptized because we had sinned. When we are baptized, we come with our imperfect, sinful lives and are baptized into His perfection. We go to Him with our unrighteousness and are baptized into His righteousness. We come as unholy and are baptized into His holiness.

Jesus and the infilling of the Holy Spirit

QUESTION **8** What two significant things happened at the baptism of Jesus?

When He had been baptized, Jesus came up immediately from the water; and behold, the heavens were opened to Him, and He saw the Spirit of God descending like a dove and alighting upon Him. And suddenly a voice came from heaven, saying, "This is My beloved Son, in whom I am well pleased" (Matthew 13:16, 17).

a. _____

b. _____

Although we may not hear an audible voice at baptism, we can be confident that the Father speaks the same assurance into our hearts, "You are My beloved child in whom I am well pleased." As children of God, we become heirs with Christ. The riches of heaven are ours. The Father offers the treasures of eternity to His sons and daughters.

The apostle Paul testifies to this eternal truth in Romans 8:16, 17: "The Spirit Himself bears witness with our spirit that we are children of God, and if children, then heirs—heirs of God and joint heirs with Christ, if indeed we suffer with Him, that we may also be glorified together."

Ellen White quotes the Father's words to Christ at His baptism and expands on this theme.

"This is My beloved Son, in whom I am well pleased," embraces humanity.

God spoke to Jesus as our representative. With all our sins and weaknesses, we are not cast aside as worthless. "He hath made us accepted in the Beloved." Ephesians 1:6. The glory that rested upon Christ is a pledge of the love of God for us. It tells us of the power of prayer,—how the human voice may reach the ear of God, and our petitions find acceptance in the courts of heaven. By sin, earth was cut off from heaven, and alienated from its communion; but Jesus has connected it again with the sphere of glory. His love has encircled man, and reached the highest heaven. The light which fell from the open portals upon the head of our Saviour will fall upon us as we pray for help to resist temptation. The voice which spoke to Jesus says to every believing soul, This is My beloved child, in whom I am well pleased.[7]

At His baptism, Christ received the divine anointing of the Holy Spirit. What does this mean? What significance does the infilling of the Holy Spirit at Christ's baptism have? He was conceived in the womb of Mary by the Holy Spirit. He was guided by the Holy Spirit throughout His childhood and impressed by the Spirit in the lessons His mother taught Him. The rabbis in the temple noticed clarity and power in His teaching in the temple when He was twelve years old that could only have come through the Holy Spirit. The infilling of the Holy Spirit at baptism strengthened Him for the temptations ahead and was His divine anointing for His three-and-a-half-year ministry. The promise of being filled with the Holy Spirit at baptism is given to all who enter the waters.

QUESTION **9** What promise is made to those who repent and are baptized?

Then Peter said to them, "Repent, and let every one of you be baptized in the name of Jesus Christ for the remission of sins; and you shall receive the gift of the Holy Spirit" (Acts 2:38).

At baptism, we receive additional strength through the Holy Spirit to face the temptations of Satan. The Holy Spirit also imparts spiritual gifts for service at our baptism. Therefore, we can claim by faith the power of the Holy Spirit given to us at baptism to overcome every temptation. We have also been equipped through the gifts of the Spirit to serve Christ and His church. This is an exciting reality that we do not want to pass over too quickly.

If you have been baptized by immersion already, at your baptism Christ has given you the guarantee or pledge of His Spirit; you are a child of God. All the riches of heaven are yours. Christ by "His divine power has given to us all things that pertain to life and godliness, through the knowledge of Him who called us by glory and virtue" (2 Peter 1:3).

Through the indwelling of the Holy Spirit, we can face every temptation that Satan throws at us. We can have the strength to meet any trial. The Third Person of the Godhead is there to encourage, strengthen, guide, instruct, and empower us. He also imparts gifts, talents, and abilities so we can serve effectively in the cause of Christ.

Baptism is a very important event in the life of the Christian. Jesus says, "He who believes and is baptized will be saved; but he who does not believe will be condemned" (Mark 16:16). Jesus considered baptism so important that He was baptized as an example for us. "Here are presented two requirements made of those who accept the gospel proclamation—faith in Jesus, and baptism. The first is the inward acceptance of the salvation so graciously provided by the vicarious death of the world's Redeemer; the second is the outward token of an inward change of life."[8]

Many people ask, "When I am baptized, am I only baptized into Jesus, or do I become part of a church?" The Bible teaches that baptism into Christ is baptism into Christ's body, the church. You can't separate the Head from the body. When we are baptized, we do not become spiritual orphans. Three thousand were baptized on the day of Pentecost and "those who gladly received his word were baptized; and that day about three thousand souls were added to them. And they continued steadfastly in the apostles' doctrine and fellowship, in the breaking of bread, and prayers" (Acts 2:41, 42).

To emphasize this point, Luke adds, "And the Lord added to the church daily those who were being saved" (Acts 2:47). From these passages, it becomes obvious that those baptized were baptized into the apostles' doctrine and fellowship and became part of the New Testament church.

Jesus commissioned His disciples to "make disciples of all the nations, baptizing them in the name of the Father and of the Son and of

93

the Holy Spirit, teaching them to observe all things that I have commanded you; and lo, I am with you always, even to the end of the age" (Matthew 28:19, 20).

The New Testament believers were baptized into Christ-centered, Bible-believing, commandment-keeping churches. And filled with their newfound faith, they went out to change the world. Once again, in this generation, God has a Christ-centered, Bible-believing, commandment-keeping church that He has called to go out and prepare the world for His soon return.

When the grace of Christ changes our hearts and we discover the truths of His Word, we long to follow Him into the waters of baptism. When Paul accepted Christ on the Damascus road, he was not left alone. The Holy Spirit directed Ananias, a devout Jewish convert, to him. Ananias instructed Paul and then said, "And now why are you waiting? Arise and be baptized, and wash away your sins, calling on the name of the Lord" (Acts 22:16).

Today, Jesus is appealing to each of us to commit our lives to Him. He is appealing to us to become part of His Bible-believing, commandment-keeping people. He gives us the same invitation He gave the apostle Paul, "Arise and be baptized." If you would like to accept His invitation, check the following boxes:

☐ I choose to follow Jesus' example of baptism and desire to be baptized soon.

☐ I choose to use the gifts that the Holy Spirit has given me for the upbuilding of Christ's church and the advancement of His kingdom.

---

1. Ellen G. White, *The Story of Redemption* (Washington, DC: Review and Herald®, 1980), 198.

2. Ellen G. White, *The Desire of Ages* (Nampa, ID: Pacific Press®, 2005), 135.

3. White, 100.

4. Francis D. Nichol, ed., *Seventh-day Adventist Bible Commentary*, vol. 5 of the Commentary Reference Series (Washington, DC: Review and Herald®, 1980), 908.

5. White, *Desire of Ages*, 104.

6. White, 111.

7. White, 113.

8. Nichol, *Seventh-day Adventist Bible Commentary*, vol. 5, 659.

LESSON 7

Jesus' Temptations and Victory

Immediately after Jesus was baptized, the Holy Spirit led Jesus into the wilderness to be tempted by the devil (see Matthew 4:1). Jesus never consciously placed Himself in a position of temptation. He did not invite temptation or willingly venture on Satan's enchanted ground.

In this instance, He was entering the wilderness to be alone with the Father to pray and prepare for His earthly ministry. It was there in the wilderness that the devil attacked Jesus with his fiercest temptations.

When Jesus faced Satan's temptations, His Father's assurance, "This is My beloved Son, in whom I am well pleased" (Matthew 3:17), was still foremost in His mind. In Christ, the Father established an everlasting connection with humanity. "Ever since Adam's sin; the human race had been cut off from direct communion with God; the intercourse between heaven and earth had been through Christ; but now that Jesus had come 'in the likeness of sinful flesh' (Romans 8:3), the Father Himself spoke. He had before communicated with humanity *through* Christ; now He communicated with humanity *in* Christ. Satan had hoped that God's abhorrence of evil would bring an eternal separation between heaven and earth. But now it was manifest

that the connection between God and man had been restored."[1]

The devil's purpose in his wilderness temptations was to get Jesus to distrust His Father and act independently of His Father's will. Jesus had just been baptized and was about to begin His ministry. Ellen White describes it this way: "When Jesus was led into the wilderness to be tempted, He was led by the *Spirit of God*. He did not invite temptation. He went to the wilderness to be alone, to contemplate His mission and work. By fasting and prayer He was to brace Himself for the bloodstained path He must travel. But Satan knew that the Saviour had gone into the wilderness, and he thought this the best time to approach Him."[2]

Jesus faced temptation in common with all humanity. He did not overcome with the strength that was inherently His as the divine Son of God. Jesus overcame by trusting in His Father to deliver Him and claiming the promises from God's Word. He came to earth to demonstrate how all humanity could be victorious through His power. Jesus came to meet temptation in the same nature that we face our temptations—human nature.

Notice these clear Bible passages:

Inasmuch then as the children have partaken of flesh and blood, He Himself likewise shared in the same, that through death He might destroy him who had the power of death, that is, the devil (Hebrews 2:14).

Therefore, in all things He had to be made like His brethren, that He might be a merciful and faithful High Priest in things pertaining to God, to make propitiation for the sins of the people (verse 17).

For we do not have a High Priest who cannot sympathize with our weaknesses, but was in all points tempted as we are, yet without sin (Hebrews 4:15).

In this lesson, we will study Christ's temptations in some detail to discover the key to victory in overcoming the temptations of the evil one.

Jesus' victory over temptation

QUESTION **1** What was Jesus' physical condition after forty days of fasting?

Just as many were astonished at you,
So His visage was marred more than any man,
And His form more than the sons of men (Isaiah 52:14).

And when He had fasted forty days and forty nights, afterward He was hungry (Matthew 4:2).

God allowed Jesus to go through the wilderness experience so that He could fully sympathize with and understand the temptations we face. He understands us because He, too, has experienced the trials, problems, and difficulties we encounter.

"Having, through His human nature, experienced the weaknesses that are common to man—though without the least taint of sin—Christ is fully sympathetic with the problems and difficulties that the sincere Christian has to face. In fact, one purpose of the incarnation was that Deity might come so close to humanity as to experience the very same problems and infirmities that are our common lot. By so doing, Christ qualified to become our High Priest and to represent us before the Father."[3]

Matthew makes it very clear that Satan's temptations came after fasting for forty days, Jesus was weak, emaciated, and hungry. It was His most vulnerable time. This was when the devil approached Him, "Weak and emaciated from hunger, worn and haggard with mental agony, 'His visage was so marred more than any man, and His form more than the sons of men.' Isaiah 52:14. Now was Satan's opportunity. Now he supposed that he could overcome Christ."[4]

In truth,

the devil always attacks us at our times of greatest weakness, for it is then we are most likely to fall. For this reason, it is of vital importance to preserve the physical, mental, and emotional powers at a high level of strength and efficiency. Anything that weakens these powers weakens our defense against the wiles of the tempter. Such things as overwork, lack of exercise, overeating, a faulty diet, lack of sleep, or anything that lessens intellectual alertness and emotional control tends to open the way for the evil one to enter the soul. . . . We must bring the body into subjection to the laws of our physical being, for it is impossible fully to appreciate things of eternal worth if we live in violation of the natural laws that govern our being.[5]

Satan followed Jesus into the wilderness and plotted to deceive Him with his most cunning temptations. The devil believed this was his best opportunity to get Jesus to distrust His Father and sin.

The devil must have been thinking about how he so effectively led Adam and Eve to sin in the garden. Satan was confident that he could get Jesus to fall as quickly as he did Adam and Eve, so he approached Jesus in His weakened state.

Jesus' first temptation—appetite

QUESTION **2** What was Jesus' first temptation in the wilderness, and why was it so significant?

Now when the tempter came to Him, he said, "If You are the Son of God, command that these stones become bread."

But He answered and said, "It is written, 'Man shall not live by bread alone, but by every word that proceeds from the mouth of God' " (Matthew 4:3, 4).

Jesus was weak, hungry, and craving food when Satan tempted Him. The stones had the appearance of bread. "With Christ, as with the holy pair in Eden, appetite was the ground of the first great temptation. Just where the ruin began, the work of our redemption must begin. As by the indulgence of appetite Adam fell, so by the denial of appetite Christ must overcome."[6] Continuing along these lines, Ellen White goes on,

So now the tempter seeks to inspire Christ with his own sentiments. "If Thou be the Son of God." The words rankle with bitterness in his mind. In the tones of his voice is an expression of utter incredulity. Would God treat His own Son thus? Would He leave Him in the desert with wild beasts, without food, without companions, without comfort? He insinuates that God never meant His Son to be in such a state as this. "If Thou be the Son of God," show Thy power by relieving Thyself of this pressing hunger. Command that this stone be made bread.[7]

Jesus' first temptation teaches us the importance of victory over appetite. This emphasis is central.

> Of all the lessons to be learned from our Lord's first great temptation *none is more important than that bearing upon the control of the appetites and passions.* In all ages, temptations appealing to the physical nature have been most effectual in corrupting and degrading mankind. Through intemperance, Satan works to destroy the mental and moral powers that God gave to man as a priceless endowment. Thus it becomes impossible for men to appreciate things of eternal worth. Through sensual indulgence, Satan seeks to blot from the soul every trace of likeness to God."[8]

All our cravings are wrapped up in Jesus' first temptation. When we struggle with the power of appetite, we can look to Jesus. He overcame Satan in the wilderness on the point of appetite.

Whatever physical cravings we face— whether for tobacco, alcohol, illicit drugs, or lustful cravings—the physical cravings that Jesus had in the wilderness after fasting for forty days were greater. Jesus understands physical cravings; He understands fleshly drives or inclinations, and His victory is our victory. In all our physical cravings, we can face Satan in the mighty, all-powerful name of Jesus and claim His victory as our own.

It is essential to overcome the temptation of appetite. If we trust God for victory over our fleshly cravings and gain victory in His strength, we can then overcome every other temptation of Satan. Furthermore, "the controlling power of appetite will prove the ruin of thousands, when, if they had

conquered on this point, they would have had moral power to gain the victory over every other temptation of Satan."[9]

Jesus' victory is our victory. Just as Satan tested Jesus on appetite, he comes to us with the same temptations. It is possible to overcome them. We don't have to wish for victory. We do not have to hope for victory, and we do not have to beg Jesus for victory as if He did not want to give it to us. We can overcome when we claim Christ's victory as our own and believe it is ours through Christ. With the apostle Paul, we can say, "I can do all things through Christ who strengthens me" (Philippians 4:13). "Jesus says, 'He hath nothing in Me.' His victory is an assurance that we too may come off victors in our conflicts with the enemy."[10] Jesus' victory is our victory. He overcame every temptation that is possible for us to face.

Jesus lived for the Father's glory, not His own. John recorded Jesus' testimony: "And He who sent Me is with Me. The Father has not left Me alone, for I always do those things that please Him" (John 8:29). Jesus has not left us alone either; He is always with us. However, we must choose to do God's will just as Jesus did. Jesus answered Satan with these words, "It is written, 'Man shall not live by bread alone, but by every word that proceeds from the mouth of God' " (Matthew 4:4).

Christ met Satan with the Word of God. There is power in God's Word. Filling our minds with the promises of Scripture will provide us with life-changing power to overcome the temptations of Satan.

Jesus' second temptation—presumption

QUESTION **3** What was Jesus' second temptation from Satan, and why was it so significant?

Then the devil took Him up into the holy city, set Him on the pinnacle of the temple, and said to Him, "If You are the Son of God, throw Yourself down. For it is written:

'He shall give His angels charge over you' " (Matthew 4:5, 6).

The devil approached Jesus a second time. This time he quoted scripture. "But again the temptation is prefaced with the insinuation of distrust, *'If Thou be the Son of God.'* Christ was tempted to answer the 'if;' but 'He refrained from the slightest acceptance of the doubt. He would not imperil His life in order to give evidence to Satan."[11]

Jesus' second temptation teaches us to take all Scripture in its context. Don't be deceived by Satan's distortion of Scripture. He quoted only part of the Scripture. "When Satan quoted the promise, 'He shall give His angels charge over Thee,' he omitted the words, 'to keep Thee in all Thy ways;' that is, in all the ways of God's choosing. Jesus refused to go outside the path of obedience. While manifesting perfect trust in His Father, He would not place Himself, unbidden, in a position that would necessitate the interposition of His Father to save Him from death. He would not force Providence to come to His rescue, and thus fail of giving man an example of trust and submission."[12]

We need to be careful that we don't distort the Scripture by using it out of context. Many are deceived because they see only part of Scripture, not Scripture in its full meaning. To understand what the Bible says on a given topic, be sure to search out everything it says on that topic. Don't jump to conclusions too quickly merely because a friend or religious leader quotes part of a text. It is helpful as well to study the entire context of the passage. What comes before and after it makes a significant difference in getting our understanding correct. The devil knows Scripture well and will quote it to his own advantage.

In the last days of earth's history, we would do well to heed these words: "None but those who have fortified the mind with the truths of the Bible will stand through the last great conflict."[13] And "only those who have been diligent students of the Scriptures and who have received the love of the truth will be shielded from the powerful delusion that takes the world captive."[14]

We will not be tempted above that which we can bear. It's easy to question God's leading when we face difficult circumstances. During tough times, it is comforting to remember that it was the Spirit of God who lead Jesus into the wilderness where He was tempted by Satan. We must trust that God is using even our most difficult times to grow us into His likeness. God is faithful to His promises, and He has promised, "No temptation has overtaken you except such as is common to man; but God is faithful, who will not allow you to be tempted beyond what you are able, but with the temptation will also make the way of escape, that you may be able to bear it" (1 Corinthians 10:13).

God measures every test that comes to us. He will not allow us to be tempted beyond what we can handle through His grace and by His power. He gives us this divine assurance that He will be by our side to strengthen us in every trial and enable us to overcome as He overcame.

Jesus' third temptation—love of the world

QUESTION **4** What was Jesus' third temptation by Satan, and why was it so significant?

Again, the devil took Him up on an exceedingly high mountain, and showed Him all the kingdoms of the world and their glory. And he said to Him, "All these things I will give You if You will fall down and worship me."

Then Jesus said to him, "Away with you, Satan! For it is written, 'You shall worship the LORD your God, and Him only you shall serve' " (Matthew 4:8–10).

This temptation was significant because Satan showed Jesus all the kingdoms of the world and their glory. He offered Him all the splendor of this world, including religious and political control. But Jesus is the true Owner of this world based on the fact that He created

all things (John 1:3). The psalmist stated,

> The earth is the LORD's and all its fullness,
> The world and those who dwell therein.
> For He has founded it upon the seas,
> And established it upon the waters (Psalm 24:1, 2).

Satan offered Jesus something that was already His.

> Placing Jesus upon a high mountain, Satan caused the kingdoms of the world, in all their glory, to pass in panoramic view before Him. . . . The eyes of Jesus, so lately greeted by gloom and desolation, now gazed upon a scene of unsurpassed loveliness and prosperity. Then the tempter's voice was heard: "All this power will I give Thee, and the glory of them: for that is delivered unto me; and to whomsoever I will I give it. If Thou therefore wilt worship me, all shall be Thine."[15]

It was not Christ's mission or purpose to gain earthly possessions, wealth, or power. Satan tempted Jesus by offering Him the entire world, but Jesus already owns the world and everything in it. Satan offered Jesus something that was not his to give. He offered to trade something of lesser value for something of much greater value. Christ was the divine Son of God, the Creator, Sustainer, and Ruler of the universe. Satan's strategy is to deceive us into thinking that what he offers is of much more value than what Jesus offers us. Jesus says in Matthew 6:33, "But seek first the kingdom of God and His righteousness, and all these things shall be added to you." Satan offers us the fading pleasures of this world, while Jesus offers us the lasting treasures of eternity.

Never give up—Jesus didn't! He will be with us in our sufferings. In all Jesus' suffering, He did not give up. There may be hardships or trials in life, but never give up. Jesus gained the victory, and through Him, we can too. "Christ's mission could be fulfilled only through suffering. Before Him was a life of sorrow, hardship, and conflict, and an ignominious death. He must bear the sins of the whole world. He must endure separation from His Father's love. Now the tempter offered to yield up the power he had usurped. Christ might deliver Himself from the dreadful future by acknowledging the supremacy of Satan. But to do this was to yield the victory in the great controversy."[16]

Jesus already owns the world; it was not Satan's to give. We face the same temptation as Jesus, so don't let the things of this world dominate your life.

QUESTION **5** How did Jesus meet Satan's temptations?

But He answered and said, "It is written, 'Man shall not live by bread alone, but by every word that proceeds from the mouth of God' " (Matthew 4:4).

When Jesus was tempted, He "met Satan with the words of Scripture. 'It is written,' He said. In every temptation the weapon of His warfare was the word of God."[17] In the same way, we can meet our temptations. "Since He gained knowledge as we may do, His intimate acquaintance with the Scriptures shows how diligently His early years were given to the study of God's word."[18]

Just as Satan tempted Jesus, he will tempt each one of us. The fact that we are tempted and have trials does not mean in any way that we are less dear to the heart of God.

Temptations are common for each one of us. Therefore, it is so important to study the life of Christ and especially His temptations to learn how we can meet the enemy and be victorious. "Many look on this conflict between Christ and Satan as having no special bearing on their own life; and for them it has little interest. But within the domain of every human heart this controversy is repeated. Never does one leave the ranks of evil for the service of God without encountering the assaults of Satan."[19]

QUESTION **6** In our fallen nature, how do we overcome the temptations of Satan?

But He answered and said, "It is written, 'Man shall not live by bread alone, but by every word that proceeds from the mouth of God' " (Matthew 4:4).

"So now, brethren, I commend you to God and to the word of His grace, which is able to build you up and give you an inheritance among all those who are sanctified" (Acts 20:32).

Grace and peace be multiplied to you in the knowledge of God and of Jesus our Lord, as His divine power has given to us all things that pertain to life and godliness, through the knowledge of Him who called us by glory and virtue, by which have been given to us exceedingly great and precious promises, that through these you may be partakers of the divine nature, having escaped the corruption that is in the world through lust (2 Peter 1:2–4).

Jesus faced Satan in the strength of the Word of God. In all three of these temptations, Jesus responded, "It is written." The Word of God can "build us up" in spiritual strength. It is through the Word that we become "partakers of the divine nature." It is through the Word that we receive heaven's power to overcome. Truly, "in our own strength it is impossible for us to deny the clamors of our fallen nature. Through this channel Satan will bring temptation upon us. Christ knew that the enemy would come to every human being, to take advantage of hereditary weakness, and by his false insinuations to ensnare all whose trust is not in God. And by passing over the ground which man must travel, our Lord has prepared the way for us to overcome."[20] Also, "we cannot save ourselves from the tempter's power; he has conquered humanity, and when we try to stand in our own strength, we shall become a prey to his devices; but 'the name of the Lord is a strong tower: the righteous runneth into it, and is safe.' Proverbs 18:10. Satan trembles and flees before the weakest soul who finds refuge in that mighty name."[21]

QUESTION **7** What was Jesus' purpose in coming to this world?

"For the Son of Man has come to seek and to save that which was lost" (Luke 19:10).

Christ came to reveal God's love to a dying, sinful planet; live the life we should have lived; and die the death we should have died. He came to redeem humanity from the clutches of sin so that we could live forever with Him in eternity.

QUESTION **8** What was Jesus' answer to Satan's last temptation?

Then Jesus said to him, "Away with you, Satan! For it is written, 'You shall worship the Lord your God, and Him only you shall serve' " (Matthew 4:10).

Although Satan would tempt Jesus throughout His entire life, Christ's course was set. He had resisted Satan in the wilderness and would face him in the strength of His Father's might throughout His life.

Fallen humanity can have the same victory over Satan's temptations as we submit ourselves to God and, in the mighty name of Jesus, choose to resist his temptations. Submitting to God and resisting the devil is the answer to overcoming Satan and all his temptations (James 4:7, 8).

QUESTION 9 Who ministered to Jesus after His temptations by Satan?

And He was there in the wilderness forty days, tempted by Satan, and was with the wild beasts; and the angels ministered to Him (Mark 1:13).

_____

_____

After the third temptation of Satan, the angels speedily ministered to Jesus. It was their part to act in the plan of salvation. When the angels heard about Christ's plan to redeem the fallen race, they offered their own lives, but only the life of the Eternal God and Creator could pay the price for a fallen world. When Jesus told them about the plan of salvation, Ellen White says,

> The angels prostrated themselves before Him. They offered their lives. Jesus said to them that He would by His death save many, that the life of an angel could not pay the debt. His life alone could be accepted of His Father as a ransom for man. Jesus also told them that they would have a part to act, to be with Him and at different times strengthen Him; that He would take man's fallen nature, and His strength would not be even equal with theirs; that they would be witnesses of His humiliation and great sufferings; and that as they would witness His sufferings, and the hatred of men toward Him, they would be stirred with the deepest emotion, and through their love for Him would wish to rescue and deliver Him from His murderers; but that they must not interfere to prevent anything they should behold; and that they should act a part in His resurrection; that the plan of salvation was devised, and His Father had accepted the plan.[22]

Angels will minister to us in all our temptations, and we will rejoice with them throughout eternity. According to Hebrews 1:14, they are "ministering spirits sent forth to minister for those who will inherit salvation." What assurance. What hope. What confidence. Heavenly angels are by our side to beat back the forces of darkness when we submit our lives to God. They are there to bring us spiritual strength in our battle with evil. They are our allies in the fight against temptation.

Jesus and the song of the redeemed

QUESTION **10** What will the song of the redeemed be because of Jesus' victorious life?

"Worthy is the Lamb who was slain
To receive power and riches and wisdom,
and strength and honor and glory and blessing!" (Revelation 5:12).

As they participate in God's plan of salvation,

all these heavenly beings have one object above all others, in which they are intensely interested—His church in a world of corruption.

All these armies are in the service of the Prince of heaven, exalting the Lamb of God, who taketh away the sins of the world. They are working for Christ under His commission, to save to the uttermost all who look to Him and believe in Him. . . .

In their service, these armies of heaven illustrate what the church of God should be. Christ is working in their behalf in the heavenly courts,

sending out His messengers to all parts of the globe, to the assistance of every suffering one who looks to Him for relief, for spiritual life and knowledge.[23]

Jesus is in the heavenly sanctuary surrounded by heavenly beings, cherubim, and seraphim—ten thousand times ten thousand angels singing "worthy is the Lamb." Our Savior and Redeemer knows our needs and understands our weakness. He is there to strengthen us, encourage us, and empower us to be overcomers. He wants us to have the same victory He had over Satan in the wilderness.

- Would you like to thank Jesus for victory over Satan?
- Would you like to make Him Master over everything in your life?
- Would you like to say, "Yes, Jesus, in Your strength, I want to resist the devil so he will flee from me"?

If that is your desire, check the box below.

☐ I desire to gain victory over every temptation, and I want Jesus to rule in my life.

---

1. Ellen G. White, *The Desire of Ages* (Nampa, ID: Pacific Press®, 2005), 116.

2. White, 114; emphasis added.

3. Francis Nichol, ed., *The Seventh-day Adventist Bible Commentary*, vol. 7 of the Commentary Reference Series (Washington DC: Review and Herald®, 1980), 426.

4. White, *Desire of Ages*, 118.

5. Francis Nichol, ed., *Seventh-day Adventist Bible Commentary*, vol. 5 of the Commentary Reference Series (Washington DC: Review and Herald®, 1980), 310.

6. White, *Desire of Ages*, 117.

7. White, 118, 119.

8. White, 122; emphasis added.

9. Ellen G. White, *Counsels on Diet and Foods* (Washington, DC: Review and Herald®, 2001), 163.

10. White, 153.

11. White, *Desire of Ages*, 124; emphasis in the original.

12. White, 125.

13. Ellen G. White, *The Great Controversy Between Christ and Satan* (Nampa, ID: Pacific Press®, 2005), 593, 594.

14. White, 625.

15. White, *Desire of Ages*, 129.

16. White, 129.

17. White, 120.

18. White, 70.

19. White, 116.

20. White, 122, 123.

21. White, 131.

22. Ellen G. White, *Early Writings* (Washington, DC: Review and Herald®, 1945), 150, 151.

23. Ellen G. White, Letter 89c, 1897.

NOTES

LESSON 8

Jesus' Ministry

John the Baptist prepared the way for Jesus' ministry. His preaching moved the multitudes to repent. Day after day, they listened to his words, and this wilderness preacher changed their lives. The people sensed that his message came from God. But they were perplexed by his statement that someone would follow him who was "mightier" (Matthew 3:11). Who was this One who was to come after John who was greater than him?

John the Baptist called Him "the Lamb of God." This title for Jesus appears in two places in the first chapter of the Gospel of John: verses 29 and 36. These two usages of the term *the Lamb of God* bracket John's testimony in verse 34, "I have seen and testified that this is the Son of God." The purpose of John's Gospel is to reveal that Jesus Christ is divine.

- His ministry reveals His divinity.
- His miracles reveal His divinity.
- His life, death, and resurrection reveal His divinity.

We read this commentary about John's declaration in *The Desire of Ages,* "Again the face of the prophet was lighted up with glory from the Unseen, as he cried, 'Behold the Lamb of God!' The words thrilled the hearts of the disciples. They did not fully understand them."[1]

Jesus anointed for ministry

At His baptism, Jesus was anointed by the Holy Spirit for His God-appointed ministry. The Holy Spirit was given to empower Him for His mission. "The word which God sent to the children of Israel, preaching peace through Jesus Christ—He is Lord of all—that word you know, which was proclaimed throughout all Judea, and began from Galilee after the baptism which John preached: how God anointed Jesus of Nazareth with the Holy Spirit and with power, who went about doing good and healing all who were oppressed by the devil, for God was with Him" (Acts 10:36–38).

Jesus was anointed with the Holy Spirit at His baptism—the public recognition of His Messianic role in the plan of God.

Immediately after His baptism, Jesus entered the wilderness to prepare for His Messianic mission. Satan recognized Jesus' divinity and attempted to destroy His ministry by leading Him into temptation. In the face

---

Some of the material in this lesson is taken from previously published Bible studies, articles, and presentations by the authors.

of the fiercest temptations, Jesus remained faithful to His divine calling. After Satan left the wilderness, Jesus was exhausted and fell to the earth. Heavenly angels comforted Him after observing the Savior's conflict in the wilderness.

> The angels now ministered to the Son of God as He lay like one dying. He was strengthened with food, comforted with the message of His Father's love and the assurance that all heaven triumphed in His victory. . . .
>
> Never can the cost of our redemption be realized until the redeemed shall stand with the Redeemer before the throne of God. Then as the glories of the eternal home burst upon our enraptured senses we shall remember that Jesus left all this for us, that He not only became an exile from the heavenly courts, but for us took the risk of failure and eternal loss. Then we shall cast our crowns at His feet, and raise the song, "Worthy is the Lamb that was slain to receive power, and riches, and wisdom, and strength, and honor, and glory, and blessing." Revelation 5:12.[2]

After this wilderness experience, Jesus began His ministry.

Jesus calls His disciples

Two of John the Baptist's followers, John and Andrew, were impressed by his announcement that Christ was the Lamb of God, and they sought out Jesus. "These were Christ's first disciples. Moved by an irresistible impulse, they followed Jesus,—anxious to speak with Him, yet awed and silent, lost in the overwhelming significance of the thought, 'Is this the Messiah?' "[3]

After finding Jesus, Andrew immediately found his brother and brought him to Jesus too. "He first found his own brother Simon, and said to him, 'We have found the Messiah' (which is translated, the Christ). And he brought him to Jesus" (John 1:41, 42).

Andrew was the first disciple to bring someone to Jesus. "Andrew sought to impart the joy that filled his heart. Going in search of his brother Simon, he cried, 'We have found the Messias.' Simon waited for no second bidding. He also had heard the preaching of John the Baptist, and he hastened to the Saviour. The eye of Christ rested upon him, reading his character and his life history. His impulsive nature, his loving, sympathetic heart, his ambition and self-confidence, the history of his fall, his repentance, his labors, and his martyr death,—the Saviour read it all."[4]

Jesus ministers to all of us. He knows us intimately. Although we may stumble and fall, He picks us up and accepts us where we are. Jesus knew Peter's future failings, yet He chose him as one of His close disciples. Eventually, Peter was changed by Christ's love and became a mighty worker for his Lord and Savior.

Next, "Jesus wanted to go to Galilee, and He found Philip and said to him, 'Follow Me.' Now Philip was from Bethsaida, the city of Andrew and Peter. Philip found Nathanael and said to him, 'We have found Him of whom Moses in the law, and also the prophets, wrote—Jesus of Nazareth, the son of Joseph' " (verses 43–45).

These were the first disciples. "John directed two of his disciples to Christ. Then one of these, Andrew, found his brother, and called him to the Saviour. Philip was then called, and he went in search of Nathanael. These examples should teach us the importance of personal effort, of making direct appeals to our kindred, friends, and neighbors."[5]

When we come to Jesus, we, too, will tell others about the Savior. Just as Andrew found his brother, Simon Peter, and brought him to Jesus, Philip found a friend and brought him to the Messiah. The book *Steps to Christ* states this truth succinctly: "No sooner does one come to Christ than there is born in his heart a desire to make known to others what a precious friend he has found in Jesus; the saving and sanctifying truth cannot be shut up in his heart."[6]

The founding of the Christian church began with the calling of John, Andrew, Simon Peter, Philip, and Nathanael. Every Christian who accepts Jesus and becomes part of His church has both the privilege and the responsibility of sharing Him with others.

When we share the message of Jesus with others, we have a greater desire to become like Him. Our character is changed into His image. Truly, "God could have reached His object in saving sinners without our aid; but in order for us to develop a character like Christ's, we must share in His work. In order to enter into His joy,—the joy of seeing souls redeemed by His sacrifice,—we must participate in His labors for their redemption."[7]

Jesus' first miracle

Every miracle that Christ performed had a deeper purpose. His entire ministry revealed the Father's love. Each act of His life demonstrated the Father's care.

QUESTION **1** What was the first miracle Jesus performed to begin His ministry?

On the third day there was a wedding in Cana of Galilee, and the mother of Jesus was there. Now both Jesus and His disciples were invited to the wedding. And when they ran out of wine, the mother of Jesus said to Him, "They have no wine."

Jesus said to her, "Woman, what does your concern have to do with Me? My hour has not yet come."

His mother said to the servants, "Whatever He says to you, do it."

Now there were set there six waterpots of stone, according to the manner of purification of the Jews, containing twenty or thirty gallons apiece. Jesus said to them, "Fill the waterpots with water." And they filled them up to the brim. And He said to them, "Draw some out now, and take it to the master of the feast." And they took it. When the master of the feast had tasted the water that was made wine, and did not know where it came from (but the servants who had drawn the water knew), the master of the feast called the bridegroom. And he said to him, "Every man at the beginning sets out the good wine, and when the guests have well drunk, then the inferior. You have kept the good wine until now!" (John 2:1–10).

Jesus' first miracle may seem like a humble beginning, but it strengthened the faith of His newly chosen disciples. "Jesus did not begin His ministry by some great work before the

Sanhedrin at Jerusalem. At a household gathering in a little Galilean village His power was put forth to add to the joy of a wedding feast. Thus He showed His sympathy with men, and His desire to minister to their happiness."[8]

In turning water into wine, Jesus met a social need. At the wedding feast at Cana, the host ran out of wine. Jesus turned the water in six stone jars into refreshing new wine and thus alleviated the host's embarrassment.

When they ran out of wine at the wedding feast, Mary told Jesus about the problem. Jesus responded to Mary, His mother, with these words. "Woman, what does your concern have to do with Me? My hour has not yet come" (John 2:4). Nevertheless,

> this answer, abrupt as it seems to us, expressed no coldness or discourtesy. The Saviour's form of address to His mother was in accordance with Oriental custom. It was used toward persons to whom it was desired to show respect. Every act of Christ's earthly life was in harmony with the precept He Himself had given, 'Honor thy father and thy mother.' Exodus 20:12. . . .
>
> . . . For thirty years He had been to her a loving and obedient son, and His love was unchanged; but He must now go about His Father's work.[9]

Throughout the Gospel of John, the expression "My hour has not yet come" refers to His crucifixion and death. In John 17:1, Jesus declared that His hour had finally come. Ellen White's comments on this phrase are helpful.

> The words, "Mine hour is not yet come," point to the fact that every act of Christ's life on earth was in fulfillment of the plan that had existed from

the days of eternity. . . .

> In saying to Mary that His hour had not yet come, Jesus was replying to her unspoken thought,—to the expectation she cherished in common with her people. She hoped that He would reveal Himself as the Messiah, and take the throne of Israel. But the time had not come. Not as a King, but as "a Man of Sorrows, and acquainted with grief," had Jesus accepted the lot of humanity.
>
> But though Mary had not a right conception of Christ's mission, she trusted Him implicitly. To this faith Jesus responded. It was to honor Mary's trust, and to strengthen the faith of His disciples, that the first miracle was performed.[10]

The time had not come for Jesus to be King because He must first drink of the cup of sorrow dying on the cross. He must bear the guilt and shame of all humanity, and "taste death for everyone" (Hebrews 2:9). This first miracle pointed forward to Christ's death. He would change the tasteless water of Judaism into the sweet wine of the gospel.

Although she did not fully understand, Mary said to those serving, "Whatever He says to you, do it" (John 2:5).

So Jesus told the servants to " 'fill the waterpots with water.' And they filled them up to the brim. And He said to them, 'Draw some out now, and take it to the master of the feast' " (verses 7, 8).

After the servants finished filling the water pots, they took some to the master of the feast. And, "when the master of the feast had tasted the water that was made wine, and did not know where it came from (but the servants who had drawn the water knew), the master of the feast called the bridegroom. And he said

to him, 'Every man at the beginning sets out the good wine, and when the guests have well drunk, then the inferior. You have kept the good wine until now!' " (verses 9, 10).

If the wine that Christ made at the wedding feast of Galilee was fermented, the symbolism of His sinless blood shed for the world would have been distorted. Also, Jesus would not create a beverage that would confuse the thinking of human beings and affect their conscience, reason, and judgment. Such a drink would make them less likely to resist temptation and more likely to sin. Instead,

> The gift of Christ to the marriage feast was a symbol. The water represented baptism into His death; the wine, the shedding of His blood for the sins of the world. The water to fill the jars was brought by human hands, but the word of Christ alone could impart to it life-giving virtue. . . .
>
> The wine which Christ provided for the feast, and that which He gave to the disciples as a symbol of His own blood, was the pure juice of the grape. . . .
>
> It was Christ who in the Old Testament gave the warning to Israel, "Wine is a mocker, strong drink is raging: and whosoever is deceived thereby is not wise." Proverbs 20:1. And He Himself provided no such beverage. . . . Christ did not contradict His own teaching. The unfermented wine which He provided for the wedding guests was a wholesome and refreshing drink. Its effect was to bring the taste into harmony with a healthful appetite.[11]

The Scriptures give us clear advice about wine. Alcohol is a significant risk factor in car accidents, abuse, and a host of other social problems. It is addictive and seriously affects our cognitive thinking processes, as well as our overall health.

Christ's first miracle powerfully demonstrated that He was the Messiah. John states, "This beginning of signs Jesus did in Cana of Galilee, and manifested His glory; and His disciples believed in Him" (John 2:11). The first miracles of Jesus strengthened the disciples' faith and belief. This enabled them to withstand the opposition of the priests and rabbis.

Jesus' comprehensive ministry

Jesus was always more interested in the needs of others than His own needs. He was concerned about them. In John's Gospel, Jesus demonstrated His immense care for the people by ministering to a variety of their needs.

When Jesus' first two disciples followed Him at a distance, He simply asked them, "What do you seek?" (John 1:38). These four words were Jesus' missionary model. He was more concerned about others' needs than His own. He was sensitive to what was taking place in their lives. By His looks, words, and actions, He constantly reached out to meet the needs of others. His life was poured out in selfless service. The Gospel of John reveals a Christ who meets our physical, mental, social, and spiritual needs.

John 2—Jesus meets a social need. His first miracle shows Christ's willingness to care for people's needs. Jesus fulfilled the need of the present moment. He prevented the embarrassment of the host at the wedding feast in Cana, sparing him from public shame.

John 3—Jesus meets a spiritual need. In John 3, we find Christ talking with a Pharisee who asked for a meeting at night. Nicodemus had become aware that he needed more than a formal religion. He was looking for something more than ritual or tradition. Jesus showed him exactly what he was looking for and how to get it. Only the Holy Spirit could change Nicodemus's heart and give him the new life

he so desperately longed for.

John 4—Jesus meets an emotional need. In John 4, Jesus encountered the woman at the well. He met her need very skillfully by giving her a measure of respect. This woman had gone through five husbands. Jesus offered this social outcast emotional support. He was kind to her and offered her something wonderful—a genuine, divine, pure love that would fill her heart and quench her inner thirst. The water of eternal life that He offered would satisfy her soul and fill her heart with joy.

John 5—Jesus meets a physical need. In John 5, Jesus performed a dramatic healing by the pool of Bethesda. Again, Jesus was meeting a person precisely at the point of his present need. The man by the pool of Bethesda was desperate. He was sick and had little hope of recovery. A cripple for thirty-eight years, he lay by the pool, longing for healing. And then Jesus came. Christ looked with compassion on this poor sufferer and reached out to him with miraculous healing.

Just as Jesus met people's needs in His day, He meets our needs today. We can depend on Him.

Jesus' popularity

Jesus' popularity reached a crescendo in John 6. He so miraculously met the perceived and real needs of thousands of people that they wanted to make Him king. The peak of His public favor came when He multiplied five loaves and two fishes on a hillside in Galilee. On this occasion, Jesus preached His timeless sermon on the bread of life. In it, He shared the cost of true discipleship. John's Gospel records the masses' response to His message: "From that time many of His disciples went back and walked with Him no more" (John 6:66).

Jesus spoke to His followers and said, "I say to you, unless you eat the flesh of the Son of Man and drink His blood, you have no life in you." This was difficult for them to understand. It marked a turning point in Jesus' ministry. Up until then, He had been widely accepted as a popular teacher and miracle-working prophet. But at this time, many of His followers left Him. The shadow of the cross lay before Him. Then Jesus asked the twelve disciples, "Do you also want to go away?" (verse 67). In other words, "Are you going to leave Me also? Are you going with the crowd? Do you still want to follow Me?"

Although many followers left and no longer followed Jesus, "Simon Peter answered Him, 'Lord, to whom shall we go? You have the words of eternal life. Also we have come to believe and know that You are the Christ, the Son of the living God' " (verses 68, 69). Their knowledge and belief were based on the miracles and ministry they had witnessed and experienced. The disciples were sure that Jesus was the long-awaited Messiah. "The Greek verb may be translated, 'we have found out,' implying that they had already learned the truth here, and still believed it to be true in spite of the many who now rejected Jesus. Peter, speaking for the Twelve, declared that not only had they had faith that Jesus was the Messiah, but also, because of the miracles they had seen and the words they had heard, they now could say that they knew He was the Son of God."[12]

Jesus' threefold ministry

Jesus came to this world to restore humanity to His image. He came to give humanity the health of body, mind, and soul. Jesus came to provide physical health, peace of mind, and perfection of character. He came as a Servant, and His ministry was complete and practical. His method is simply this:

1 To reach people where they are
2 To touch people at the point of their present need

3 To give people a glimpse of His magnificent love

Jesus' method of evangelism will revolutionize your life, and it will transform our church. Our Lord's strategy is summed up in the following statement, "Christ's method alone will give true success in reaching the people. The Saviour mingled with men as one who desired their good. He showed His sympathy for them, ministered to their needs, and won their confidence. Then He bade them, 'Follow Me.' "[13]

Every day we rub shoulders with people who have all kinds of needs—physical, emotional, mental, and spiritual. Christ is eager to meet those needs through us as we show concern for people's loneliness, sorrow, and heartaches. As we show an interest in their felt needs, their hearts will be touched.

QUESTION **2** What was the threefold ministry of Jesus?

And Jesus went about all Galilee, teaching in their synagogues, preaching the gospel of the kingdom, and healing all kinds of sickness and all kinds of disease among the people (Matthew 4:23).

The teaching, preaching, and healing ministry of Jesus summarizes the totality of Jesus' ministry. Jesus' ministry encompasses the mind, soul, and body.

Mind—Teaching
Soul—Preaching
Body—Healing

During Jesus' ministry, He spent more time healing the sick than preaching. However, He used each work of healing as an opportunity for implanting divine principles in the mind and soul. "The Saviour made each work of healing an occasion for implanting divine principles in the mind and soul. This was the purpose of His work."[14] Jesus longed for people to be whole and complete.

Jesus was interested in more than opening blind eyes. He longed for people to see *divine realities*.

Jesus was interested in more than opening deaf ears. He longed for people to hear *divine truth*.

Jesus was interested in more than healing diseased bodies. He longed for people to be restored to the *divine image*.

Jesus desired to show that divine healing is performed not only to heal but also to save. His miracles testified of His divine power and led people to believe in the Source of that divine power. Many who were healed by Jesus listened to the preaching of the apostles and accepted His offer of salvation. "At the crucifixion of Christ, those who had thus been healed did not join with the rabble throng in crying, 'Crucify Him, crucify Him.' Their sympathies were with Jesus; for they had felt His great sympathy and wonderful power. They knew Him to be their Saviour; for He had given them health of body and soul. They listened to the preaching of the apostles, and the entrance of God's word into their hearts gave them understanding. They became agents of God's mercy, and instruments of His salvation."[15]

Jesus helps us to help others

Do we have ulterior motives as we minister physically, mentally, and emotionally to people? Indeed, we do. We recognize that without Jesus, men and women will never be complete. They will never have total health. Total health includes physical, mental, emotional, and spiritual wholeness.

We are willing to help people because they are children of God, created in His image. But our interest in them prompts us to give them more than physical health. We recognize that without the spiritual, their lives will be incomplete. We want them to have the abundant life Jesus offered. We long for them to have the fullness He supplies. We are interested in the spiritual because we do not want to shortchange them. We don't want them to live below their privileges. If love prompts us to meet their physical needs, that same love will cause us to want to give them everything Jesus offers. We desire to do more than merely meet their felt needs; through Jesus, we long to supply their ultimate needs. Jesus' goal was much more than to create healthy sinners. His ultimate goal was for them to accept the message of salvation and live forever.

Jesus' impact

QUESTION **3** What was the effect of Jesus' healing ministry?

> Then His fame went throughout all Syria; and they brought to Him all sick people who were afflicted with various diseases and torments, and those who were demon-possessed, epileptics, and paralytics; and He healed them. Great multitudes followed Him—from Galilee, and from Decapolis, Jerusalem, Judea, and beyond the Jordan (Matthew 4:24, 25).

Every miracle that Christ worked had a threefold purpose:

❶ *Reveal* the Father's immense love for people and His desire to make them whole

❷ *Testify* to the fact that He was the Messiah

❸ *Break down* prejudice and open minds to receive the gospel

In truth, "Christ never worked a miracle except to supply a genuine necessity, and every miracle was of a character to lead the people to the tree of life, whose leaves are for the healing of the nations."[16]

Jesus healed sick people who were afflicted with various diseases. Many of the diseases people suffered they brought upon themselves by their sinful or unhealthful lifestyle. Yet Jesus did not turn them away. There was no limit to His compassion.

In the first chapter of Mark, Jesus left Capernaum without healing everyone in the area. Jesus chose to leave town before His popularity rose after healing scores of people. He was concerned that they would misunderstand His mission. After healing crowds of people all day, Jesus said to His disciples, "Let us go into the next towns, that I may preach there also because for this purpose I have come forth" (Mark 1:38). This passage clearly states Jesus' true purpose in ministry—He came "to seek and save that which was lost" (Luke 19:10).

QUESTION **4** What does James encourage the sick to do when they are facing a serious illness?

> Is anyone among you sick? Let him call for the elders of the church, and let them pray over him, anointing him with oil in the name of the Lord (James 5:14).

QUESTION **5** What will happen to the sick when Christ's disciples lay hands on them?

And the prayer of faith will save the sick, and the Lord will raise him up. And if he has committed sins, he will be forgiven (James 5:15).

The prayer of faith is so important. Faith is trusting God as a Friend well known, knowing that He will never harm us and always has our best interest in mind. As we pray for the sick, we can trust a God who knows the end from the beginning and always does all things right. There may be three different kinds of healing that take place:

1. *Immediate healing.* God may choose to heal the sick one immediately as He did for many in the New Testament.
2. *Gradual healing.* God may see that it is best to heal the sick one gradually. He may use the modern miracle of science or some more natural, therapeutic method.
3. *Healing in the resurrection.* It may be that our faith needs to be strengthened by the sick one resting in Jesus and being healed at the resurrection.

Ellen G. White comments on Jesus' continued healing ministry:

And Christ is the same compassionate physician now that He was during His earthly ministry. In Him there is healing balm for every disease, restoring power for every infirmity. His disciples in this time are to pray for the sick as verily as the disciples of old prayed. And recoveries will follow; for the "the prayer of faith shall save the sick." We have the Holy Spirit's power, the calm assurance of faith, that can claim God's promises. The Lord's promise, "They shall lay hands on the sick and they shall recover" (Mark 16:18), is just as trustworthy now as in the days of the apostles. It represents the privilege of God's children, and our faith should lay hold of all that it embraces.[17]

And,

I saw that the reason why God did not hear the prayers of His servants for the sick among us more fully was, that He could not be glorified in so doing while they were violating the laws of health. And I also saw that He designed the health reform and Health Institute to prepare the way for the prayer of faith to be fully answered. Faith and good works should go hand in hand in relieving the afflicted among us, and in fitting them to glorify God here, and to be saved at the coming of Christ.[18]

Jesus doesn't heal everyone

QUESTION **6** What are some of the reasons that Jesus doesn't heal everyone who asks Him for healing?

So Jesus said to them, "Because of your unbelief; for assuredly, I say to you, if you have faith as a mustard seed, you will say to this mountain, 'Move from here to there,' and it will move; and nothing will be impossible for you" (Matthew 17:20).

If I regard iniquity in my heart, the Lord will not hear (Psalm 66:18).

Concerning this thing I pleaded with the Lord three times that it might depart from me. And He said to me, "My grace is sufficient for you, for My strength is made perfect in weakness" (2 Corinthians 12:8, 9).

Again, let's look at Ellen White's comments on healing:

Many have expected that God would keep them from sickness merely because they have asked Him to do so. But God did not regard their prayers, because their faith was not made

perfect by works. God will not work a miracle to keep those from sickness who have no care for themselves, but are continually violating the laws of health, and make no efforts to prevent disease. When we do all we can on our part to have health, then may we expect that the blessed results will follow, and we can ask God in faith to bless our efforts for the preservation of health. He will then answer our prayer, if His name can be glorified thereby.[19]

Jesus invites His followers to participate with Him in ministry today. He is our Example.

The poor are to be relieved, the sick cared for, the sorrowing and bereaved comforted, the ignorant instructed, the inexperienced counseled. . . .

We should ever remember that the object of the medical missionary work is to point sin-sick men and women to the Man of Calvary, who taketh away the sin of the world. By beholding Him,

they will be changed into His likeness. We are to encourage the sick and suffering to look to Jesus and live.[20]

Jesus calls us to follow His pattern

Jesus had an effective ministry of teaching, preaching, and healing (Matthew 4:23). When we combine this threefold ministry, there will be amazing, unusual, and powerful results in our ministry as well. The Lord spoke clearly to Ellen White regarding this threefold ministry:

If ever the Lord has spoken by me, He speaks when I say that the workers engaged in educational lines, in ministerial lines, and in medical missionary lines must stand as a unit, all laboring under the supervision of God, one helping the other, each blessing each. . . .

Christ, the great Medical Missionary, is our example. . . . He healed the sick and preached the gospel. In His service, healing and teaching were linked closely together. Today they are not to be separated.[21]

QUESTION **7** Why were the miracles of Jesus recorded by the inspired writers?

And truly Jesus did many other signs in the presence of His disciples, which are not written in this book; but these are written that you may believe that Jesus is the Christ, the Son of God, and that believing you may have life in His name (John 20:30, 31).

The miracles that Jesus performed were so that men and women would believe that He is the Christ, the Son of God. If you believe He is the Divine Son of God, and trust Him fully and want to be involved in His ministry, check the box below.

☐ I want to be actively involved in some part of Jesus' threefold ministry.

1. Ellen G. White, *The Desire of Ages* (Nampa, ID: Pacific Press®, 2005), 138.

2. White, 131.

3. White, 138.

4. White, 139.

5. White, 141.

6. Ellen G. White, *Steps to Christ* (Washington, DC: Review and Herald®, 1977), 78.

7. White, *Desire of Ages,* 142.

8. White, 144.

9. White, 146, 147.

10. White, 147.

11. White, 148, 149.

12. Francis D. Nichol, ed., *Seventh-day Adventist Bible Commentary*, vol. 5 of the Commentary Reference Series (Washington DC: Review and Herald®, 1980), 973.

13. Ellen G. White, *The Ministry of Healing* (Mountain View, CA: Pacific Press®, 1942), 143.

14. White, 20.

15. White, *Desire of Ages*, 163.

16. White, 366.

17. White, *Ministry of Healing*, 226.

18. Ellen G. White, *Counsels on Diet and Foods* (Washington, DC: Review and Herald®, 1938), 25, 26.

19. White, 26.

20. White, 458, 459.

21. Ellen G. White, *Testimonies for the Church*, vol. 9 (Mountain View, CA: Pacific Press®, 1948), 169–171.

NOTES

LESSON 9

Jesus' Worship

God created us as worshiping beings. We all will worship something. Some worship fashion; others have their sports or entertainment idols. Still others worship the gods of money and materialism. These superficial objects of worship do not satisfy the deepest longings of the human heart.

Only the One who made us knows how to make us genuinely happy. He has made us to have deep joy, inner purpose, and lasting peace in and through worshiping Him. Jesus is our Example in true worship. In this lesson, we will explore Christ's model of authentic worship and discover the keys to living life in all its abundance. With this in mind, we must ask ourselves three questions:

- What is true worship?
- What were Jesus' worship practices?
- What can we apply from Jesus' worship habits to our worship practices today?

This lesson focuses on how, when, and where Jesus worshiped and the importance of worshiping Jesus as our Creator. Let's carefully review Jesus' worship practices.

Jesus' worship practices

QUESTION **1** What was Jesus' practice on the Sabbath?

> So He came to Nazareth, where He had been brought up. And as His custom was, He went into the synagogue on the Sabbath day, and stood up to read (Luke 4:16).

_____

_____

Jesus' practice was to attend the synagogue on the Sabbath and read from the Scriptures. His positive example to us is a model of true worship. In the Jewish synagogues of the first century, hymns were sung in praise to God, the Old Testament Scriptures were read, and prayers were offered. Jesus participated in these three elements of worship—song, Bible study, and prayer. Sabbath worship was also a time of close fellowship. Friendships were deepened, and a religious community of mutual support was created.

Jesus fulfills Isaiah's prophecy

In the synagogue on Sabbath, any male Israelite might give the Sabbath reading from the prophets. On one Sabbath, Jesus was asked to take part in the service.

> And He was handed the book of the prophet Isaiah. And when He had opened the book, He found the place where it was written:
>
> > "The Spirit of the LORD is upon Me,
> > Because He has anointed Me
> > To preach the gospel to the poor;
> > He has sent Me to heal the
> > brokenhearted,
> > To proclaim liberty to the captives
> > And recovery of sight to the blind,
> > To set at liberty those who are
> > oppressed;
> > To proclaim the acceptable year of the
> > LORD."
>
> Then He closed the book, and gave it back to the attendant and sat down. And the eyes of all who were in the synagogue were fixed on Him. And He began to say to them, "Today this Scripture is fulfilled in your hearing" (Luke 4:17–21).

Jesus read the very passage in Isaiah that prophesied about Him. Jesus' manner was humble and inviting.

Jesus stood before the people as a living expositor of the prophecies concerning Himself. Explaining the words He had read, He spoke of the Messiah as a reliever of the oppressed, a liberator of captives, a healer of the afflicted, restoring sight to the blind, and revealing to the world the light of truth. His impressive manner and the wonderful import of His words thrilled the hearers with a power they had never felt before. The tide of divine influence broke every barrier down; like Moses, they beheld the Invisible. As their hearts were moved upon by the Holy Spirit, they responded with fervent amens and praises to the Lord.

But when Jesus announced, "This day is this scripture fulfilled in your ears," they were suddenly recalled to think of themselves, and of the claims of Him who had been addressing them.[1]

Now, they began questioning who Jesus was. Wasn't He the carpenter's Son? They had watched as He grew from childhood to youth and then became an adult. They saw His selfless character, and they heard about His miracles. But they would not believe He was the promised Messiah.

Jesus was consistent in His worship practices every Sabbath. Matthew 13:54 records, "When He had come to His own country, He taught them in their synagogue, so that they were astonished and said, 'Where did this Man get this wisdom and these mighty works?' " Commenting on Jesus' life as an example for our lives, the apostle John states,

> He who says he abides in Him ought himself also to walk just as He walked.
> Brethren, I write no new commandment to you, but an old commandment

which you have had from the beginning. The old commandment is the word which you heard from the beginning (1 John 2:6, 7).

Christ's Sabbath-keeping example reflects God's ideal of worship for us. If we desire to "walk as He walked," we will follow His footsteps into the church for Sabbath worship.

Throughout the book of Acts, we discover that the New Testament church followed Jesus' example of Sabbath keeping (Acts 13:42–44; 16:13; 17:2). The apostle Paul encourages each New Testament believer by declaring, "And let us consider one another in order to stir up love and good works, not forsaking the assembling of ourselves together, as is the manner of some, but exhorting one another, and so much the more as you see the Day approaching" (Hebrews 10:24, 25). Sabbath worship was an integral part of the New Testament church as they followed the example of Jesus.

Jesus' activities on the Sabbath

Jesus kept the Sabbath and taught His disciples to keep the Sabbath. He was the One who made the Sabbath holy; therefore, He kept it holy and taught His disciples to keep it holy. In addition to worshiping on the Sabbath, Jesus performed acts of mercy and kindness that reflected the character of God and drew hearts to the redemptive power of the gospel.

QUESTION **2** What were some of the activities Jesus did on the Sabbath?

They brought him who formerly was blind to the Pharisees. Now it was a Sabbath when Jesus made the clay and opened his eyes. Then the Pharisees also asked [the blind man] again how he had received his sight. He said to them, "He put clay on my eyes, and I washed, and I see."

Therefore some of the Pharisees said, "This Man is not from God, because He does not keep the Sabbath" (John 9:13–16).

_____

_____

Jesus performed seven of His miracles on the Sabbath. His Sabbath miracles illustrate that His intention for all people is health, wholeness, and abundant life. Each of these miracles has a deeper redemptive purpose than physical healing. In healing a man born blind, Jesus desired to show the religious leaders that He came to open spiritually blind eyes and enable people to see God clearly. His healing miracle of restoring a withered hand had a deeper spiritual purpose. He was revealing His intent to exchange stale tradition for a living faith. "And when He had looked around at them with anger, being grieved by the hardness of their hearts, He said to the man, 'Stretch out your hand.' And he stretched it out, and his hand was restored as whole as the other" (Mark 3:5). Truly, "in the healing of the withered hand, Jesus condemned the custom of the Jews, and left the fourth commandment standing as God had given it. 'It is lawful to do well on the Sabbath days,' He declared. By sweeping away the senseless restrictions of the Jews, Christ honored the Sabbath, while those who complained of Him were dishonoring God's holy day."[2]

Jesus fed the disciples on the Sabbath

Jesus also demonstrated His concern about meeting our needs by defending His disciples as they plucked grain and ate it on the Sabbath.

> Now it happened that He went through the grainfields on the Sabbath; and as they went His disciples began to pluck the heads of grain. And the Pharisees said to Him, "Look, why do they do what is not lawful on the Sabbath?"
>
> But He said to them, "Have you never read what David did when he was in need and hungry, he and those with him: how he went into the house of God in the days of Abiathar the high priest, and ate the showbread, which is not lawful to eat except for the priests, and also gave some to those who were with him?"
>
> And He said to them, "The Sabbath was made for man, and not man for the Sabbath" (Mark 2:23–27).

Furthermore, "In the days of Christ the Sabbath had become so perverted that its observance reflected the character of selfish and arbitrary men rather than the character of the loving heavenly Father. The rabbis virtually represented God as giving laws which it was impossible for men to obey. They led the people to look upon God as a tyrant, and to think that the observance of the Sabbath, as He required it, made men hard-hearted and cruel. It was the work of Christ to clear away these misconceptions."[3]

Some may ask, What about cooking on the Sabbath? Jesus was balanced in everything He did. Although the Sabbath should not be a day of arduous cooking, it is perfectly acceptable to eat food that has been prepared ahead of time and warmed up on the Sabbath. Much of the food can be made the day before Sabbath on what the Bible calls the preparation day. It has been suggested that, "While cooking upon the Sabbath should be avoided, it is not necessary to eat cold food. In cold weather let the food prepared the day before be heated. And let the meals, though simple, be palatable and attractive. Provide something that will be regarded as a treat, something the family do not have every day."[4]

The principle here is clear. Sabbath should not be a day of extensive, exhausting work. It should be a time to worship God, fellowship with our families and friends, and unselfishly serve those in need. But the object of everything we do on Sabbath is to be agents of salvation and grace. "Christ would teach His disciples and His enemies that the service of God is first of all. The object of God's work in this world is the redemption of man; therefore that which is necessary to be done on the Sabbath in the accomplishment of this work is in accord with the Sabbath law."[5]

Every act of healing, each deed of kindness, each manifestation of mercy served the larger purpose showing what God was like. These loving acts broke down the walls of prejudice and opened minds for the gospel message. Many who experienced Christ's loving ministry became His followers in the book of Acts.

QUESTION **3** How did Jesus justify acts of mercy on the Sabbath when being challenged by the Pharisees?

"Of how much more value then is a man than a sheep? Therefore it is lawful to do good on the Sabbath" (Matthew 12:12).

Jesus attempted to help the Jewish religious leaders change their priorities. They prioritized ceremonial traditions, man-made laws, and religious decrees. Jesus prioritized people. He showed sympathy for their concerns and met their needs. "Divine mercy has directed that the sick and suffering be cared for; the labor required to make them comfortable is a work of necessity, and no violation of the Sabbath. But all unnecessary work should be avoided."[6]

The heavenly hosts are keeping the Sabbath by worshiping God and ministering to our needs; heaven invites us to follow in Jesus' footsteps and do the same. "All heaven is keeping the Sabbath, but not in a listless, do-nothing way. On this day every energy of the soul should be awake, for are we not to meet with God and with Christ our Saviour? We may behold Him by faith. He is longing to refresh and bless every soul."[7]

Jesus created the Sabbath for mankind

The Sabbath is Christ's special gift to all people. Jesus created the Sabbath for us. The entire purpose of the Sabbath was to benefit everyone.

The Sabbath is God's remedy for a stress-filled world. God knew we needed the Sabbath to slow us down. He knew we needed to come apart, rest, and worship Him. So, "the Sabbath was made for man, and not man for the Sabbath" (Mark 2:27). In the very beginning, Jesus made the Sabbath as a blessing to all mankind. It is the memorial of Creation. God intended that as we worship Him from Sabbath to Sabbath, we would remember Him forever as the true and living God, the Creator of all things in heaven and earth.

The Sabbath was given by the hand of a loving Creator for our benefit, and it was reaffirmed when God presented the Ten Commandments at Mount Sinai. "God saw that a Sabbath was essential for man, even in Paradise. He needed to lay aside his own interests and pursuits for one day of the seven, that he might more fully contemplate the works of God and meditate upon His power and goodness. He needed a Sabbath to remind him more vividly of God and to awaken gratitude because all that he enjoyed and possessed came from the beneficent hand of the Creator."[8]

Jesus, the law, and the Sabbath

Jesus did not come to abolish the law He wrote with His own fingers on tables of stone. The Sabbath commandment is eternally etched on those tables as a memorial of Creation. The Creator speaks to us plainly in the fourth commandment:

Remember the Sabbath day, to keep it holy. Six days you shall labor and do all your work, but the seventh day is the Sabbath of the LORD your God. In it you shall do no work: you, nor your son, nor your daughter, nor your male servant, nor your female servant, nor your cattle, nor your stranger who is within your gates. For in six days the LORD made the heavens and the earth, the sea, and all that is in them, and rested the seventh day. Therefore, the LORD blessed the Sabbath day and hallowed it (Exodus 20:8–11).

QUESTION **4** For us to maintain a strong spiritual experience like Jesus, what does God admonish us to do on the Sabbath?

Oh come, let us worship and bow down;
Let us kneel before the LORD our Maker.
For He is our God,
And we are the people of His pasture,
And the sheep of His hand (Psalm 95:6, 7).

As we come to God's house on Sabbath, we will receive spiritual strength like Jesus. Our hearts will be refreshed, our minds renewed, and our spirits strengthened. Sabbath worship will prepare us for the challenges and trials of the coming week.

We worship Christ by coming to His sanctuary every Sabbath. Jesus' message for His people living in the last days of earth's history is a call to worship Him as the Creator.

Jesus, the Creator of the Sabbath

God calls us back to worship the Creator, Jesus Christ. The sign of His Creatorship, the memorial of Creation, is His Sabbath. When we worship each Sabbath, we give our highest allegiance to Jesus Christ. The Sabbath is a prescription given to us by the divine Physician. It is God's answer to the problems of tension and stress in an overstressed world. When Christ gave humanity the Sabbath in Eden, He stated that it would serve three specific purposes—blessing, sanctification, and rest (Genesis 2:1–4).

To *bless* something is to give it an intrinsic value that it does not have otherwise. Jesus placed within the Sabbath the special blessing of His presence for all who observe it. We meet Him again each Sabbath and experience His love and truth in fresh, new ways.

To *sanctify* is to set apart for some holy, or special, use. When we observe the day that He has set apart as sacred, He re-creates us in His image, so we become holy vessels for His use.

Jesus rested on the Sabbath at Creation, not because He was tired—but in the perfect peace of completed work. Each Sabbath, we rest in the assurance that we are one with Him. The Sabbath becomes our peaceful haven of refuge in a crazy, stressed-out world. In Christ, the Sabbath is an anchor for our soul.

We have already established in previous lessons the fact that Jesus created the heavens and the earth. However, let's confirm this fact by looking at the following texts as we expand on this idea of Jesus, Creation, and the Sabbath:

To me, who am less than the least of all the saints, this grace was given, that I should preach among the Gentiles the unsearchable riches of Christ, and to make all see what is the fellowship of the mystery, which from the beginning of the ages has been hidden in God who created all things through Jesus Christ (Ephesians 3:8, 9).

He has delivered us from the power of darkness and conveyed us into the kingdom of the Son of His love, in whom we have redemption through His blood, the forgiveness of sins.

He is the image of the invisible God, the firstborn over all creation. For by Him all things were created that are in heaven and that are on earth, visible and invisible, whether thrones or dominions or principalities or powers. All things were created through Him and for Him (Colossians 1:13–16).

All three Members of the Godhead—the Father, Son, and Holy Spirit—participated in creating planet Earth. The Sabbath is both the gift of Jesus and the special treasure of the Father and the Holy Spirit. This fact demonstrates beyond doubt that the Sabbath is not a Jewish institution. It is Christ's Sabbath.

Therefore, the New Testament records in three places that Jesus stated that He is the Lord of the Sabbath (Matthew 12:8; Mark 2:28; Luke 6:5).

The amazing book on the life of Jesus called *The Desire of Ages* says this: "All things were created by the Son of God. 'In the beginning was the Word, and the Word was with God. . . . All things were made by Him; and without Him was not anything made that was made.' John 1:1–3. And since the Sabbath is a memorial of the work of creation, it is a token of the love and power of Christ."[9]

Jesus, the Son of God, created a fantastic world. The earth, with its flowing rivers, peaceful ponds, rolling hills, majestic trees, and colorful flowers, was exceedingly beautiful as it came into existence from the hand of the Creator. On the sixth day of Creation, Jesus completed the crowning work of His hands. "So God created man in His own image; in the image of God He created him; male and female He created them" (Genesis 1:27). "And the LORD God formed man of the dust of the ground, and breathed into his nostrils the breath of life; and man became a living being" (Genesis 2:7).

What glorious, perfect beings came from the hand of our Creator! Adam was perfect! His skin glowed with health. He was full of energy and life. "When Adam came from the Creator's hand, he bore, in his physical, mental, and spiritual nature, a likeness to his Maker. 'God created man in His own image' (Genesis 1:27), and it was His purpose that the longer man lived, the more fully he should reveal this image—the more fully reflect the glory of the Creator. All his faculties were capable of development; their capacity and vigor were continually to increase."[10]

Eve was beautiful! She was a little shorter than Adam. "Eve was created from a rib taken from the side of Adam, signifying that she was not to control him as the head, nor to be trampled under his feet as an inferior, but to stand by his side as an equal, to be loved and protected by him."[11]

Our first parents were full of joy and happiness. They strolled hand in hand through the Garden, delighted in one another's love and their perfect peace. There was no discord in their home. No strain of angry voices. No stress, tension, or anxiety.

They lived in a beautiful garden among the lofty trees, beautiful flowers, colorful birds, and playful animals. Everything around them spoke of the Creator's love and desire to make them happy. Best of all, they had the glorious privilege of walking and talking face-to-face with their Creator.

The first day they spent together was the Sabbath. I can imagine that on that first Sabbath, their voices joined the angels' in highest praise to their Creator for His goodness to them. I can also imagine the heights to which their spirits soared as Jesus led out in worship that day, explaining the intricacies of nature and the mysteries of the universe.

What a Sabbath that must have been! Throughout the centuries, Jesus' people have gathered on the Sabbath to praise His name and receive spiritual strength. Jesus kept the Sabbath, and He is our Example in Sabbath keeping. One day we will join with the angels and beings from the unfallen worlds and the saints of all ages to worship Him on Sabbath.

Isaiah 66:23 declares,

"And it shall come to pass
That from one New Moon to another,
And from one Sabbath to another,
All flesh shall come to worship before Me,"
    says the LORD.

Each Sabbath through the ceaseless ages of eternity, we shall gather to sing praises to His name and worship Christ as Lord of all. We will sing with the angel choirs, "Crown Him With Many Crowns."[12]

Crown Him with many crowns,
The Lamb upon His throne;
Hark! How the heavenly anthem drowns,
All music but its own!
Awake, my soul, and sing
Of Him who died for thee,
And hail Him as thy matchless King
Through all eternity.

Crown Him the Lord of life,
Who triumphed o'er the grave,
And rose victorious in the strife
For those He came to save;
His glories now we sing
Who died and rose on high,
Who died eternal life to bring,
And lives that death may die.

Crown Him the Lord of love!
Behold His hands and side,
Those wounds, yet visible above,
In beauty glorified;
No angel in the sky
Can fully bear that sight,
But downward bends his wondering eye
At mysteries so great.

Crown Him the Lord of years,
The Potentate of time,
Creator of the rolling spheres,
Ineffably sublime!
All hail! Redeemer hail!
For Thou hast died for me;
Thy praise shall never, never fail
Throughout eternity.

If it is your desire to worship on the Sabbath, check the box below:

☐ It's my desire to worship Jesus, the Creator of heaven and earth.

1. Ellen G. White, *The Desire of Ages* (Nampa, ID: Pacific Press®, 2005), 237.
2. White, 287.
3. White, 284.
4. Ellen G. White, *Testimonies for the Church*, vol. 6 (Mountain View, CA: Pacific Press®, 1948), 357.
5. White, *Desire of Ages*, 285.
6. Ellen G. White, "A Sabbath Reform Needed," *Signs of the Times*, May 20, 1886, 1.
7. White, *Testimonies for the Church*, vol. 6, 362.
8. Ellen G. White, *Patriarchs and Prophets* (Nampa, ID: Pacific Press®, 2005), 48.
9. White, *Desire of Ages*, 281.
10. Ellen G. White, *Education* (Mountain View, CA: Pacific Press®, 1952), 15.
11. White, *Patriarchs and Prophets*, 46.
12. Matthew Bridges, "Crown Him With Many Crowns" (1851).

LESSON

Worshiping Jesus

When you think of the book of Revelation, what do you think of? Many people think of strange beasts, mystical symbols, and horrible plagues. Many Christians avoid Revelation because they think it is too difficult to understand. As one person said, "Why would I want to study Revelation? Just give me Jesus."

However, Revelation is all about Jesus. According to Revelation 1:1, it is the "Revelation of Jesus Christ." The very title of the book indicates that it is an open book, not a closed one. The word *revelation* means an unfolding or revealing. Revelation reveals the beauty of Jesus' love, the majesty of His grace, the immensity of His care, the strength of His power, and the glory of His victory over the forces of evil. The theme of Revelation is Jesus wins, Satan loses.

In this lesson, we will study Jesus' last-day message to the world. Revelation draws aside the prophetic curtain and gives us a glimpse of the past, the present, and the future. We have a box seat as we watch the greatest drama in the universe play out. But remember, we do not merely observe; we participate in this cosmic conflict between good and evil.

In our last lesson, we studied Jesus' Sabbath worship practices. We discovered that Jesus, the Creator, has given us an eternal sign of His creative authority. He has left us an example of Sabbath keeping in His own life. His final message to humanity is a call to worship Him as the Creator. This message is found in the three angels' messages of Revelation 14:6–12. It is Jesus' special, last-day message for earth's final hour. Let's take a look.

Jesus and the three angels' messages

First angel's message: "Then I saw another *angel flying* in the midst of heaven, having the everlasting gospel to preach to those who dwell on the earth—to every nation, tribe, tongue, and people—saying with a loud voice, 'Fear God and give glory to Him, for the hour of His judgment has come; and worship Him who made heaven and earth, the sea and springs of water' " (Revelation 14:6, 7; emphasis added).

Jesus' last-day message to the world is the "everlasting gospel." The word *gospel* simply means "good news." The gospel is the incredibly good news that Jesus took the initiative in our salvation. He came to earth to reveal the Father's love, live the life we should have lived, and die the death we should have died.

The Bible plainly states, "The wages of

Some of the material in this lesson is taken from previously published Bible studies, articles, and presentations by the authors.

sin is death, but the gift of God is eternal life in Christ Jesus our Lord" (Romans 6:23). Jesus bore the guilt, shame, and condemnation of our sin. He was condemned for our sins in which He had no share so we could receive His righteousness in which we had no share (see 2 Corinthians 5:21; Galatians 2:20; 3:19).

The gospel delivers us from the penalty and the power of sin. This good news of God's grace that delivers us from sin's condemnation and leads us to obedience will be preached to the ends of the earth before Jesus returns.

In His magnificent sermon on last-day signs, Jesus declared, "And this gospel of the kingdom will be preached in all the world as a witness to all the nations, and then the end will come" (Matthew 24:14).

In light of the everlasting gospel going to the ends of the earth, the first angel loudly says, "Fear God and give glory to Him, for the hour of His judgment is come; and worship Him who made heaven and earth" (Revelation 14:7). This passage has three strong verbs that are significant:

- *Fear*: To fear God is to respect Him enough to put Him first in our thinking.
- *Glorify*: To glorify God speaks of a lifestyle of commitment to His will.
- *Worship*: To worship God as the One who made heaven, earth, and the things in it is to worship Him as the Creator.

Since Jesus created the heavens and the earth, this is an appeal to honor Him by following His example in worshiping on Sabbath. The first angel makes this judgment-hour appeal near the end of earth's history.

Second angel's message: "And *another angel*

followed, saying, 'Babylon is fallen, is fallen, that great city, because she has made all nations drink of the wine of the wrath of her fornication' " (Revelation 14:8; emphasis added).

The ancient city of Babylon had long since fallen when John wrote these words. The Medo-Persian Empire overthrew Babylon in 539 B.C. John wrote nearly six hundred years later, at the end of the first century. Clearly, John is referring to a spiritual Babylon.

Spiritual Babylon represents religious confusion and an emphasis on human traditions. Nebuchadnezzar, the king of Babylon, arrogantly stated, "Is not this great Babylon, that I have built for a royal dwelling by my mighty power and for the honor of my majesty?" (Daniel 4:30). Babylon seeks glory for itself. It desires recognition, praise, and honor.

Instead, the gospel invites us to give glory to God. Believers are more interested in His honor than their own. Spiritual Babylon places human tradition above divine commands in the act of self-exaltation. The three angels' messages call us back to placing Christ in His rightful place of honor by living lives of commitment and obedience that glorify Him.

Third angel's message:

Then a *third angel* followed them, saying with a loud voice, "If anyone worships the beast and his image, and receives his mark on his forehead or on his hand, he himself shall also drink of the wine of the wrath of God, which is poured out full strength into the cup of His indignation. He shall be tormented with fire and brimstone in the presence of the holy angels and in the presence of the Lamb. And the smoke of their torment ascends forever and ever; and they have no rest day or night, who worship the beast and his image, and whoever receives the mark of his name."

Here is the patience of the saints; here are those who keep the commandments of God and the faith of Jesus (Revelation 14:9–12; emphasis added).

The three angels' messages are for people living during the final, climactic hours of earth's history. Their critical messages announce, "The hour of God's judgment has come." It is an urgent message for men and women everywhere to prepare for the soon return of Christ to planet Earth.

Worship is at the very heart of this controversy between good and evil. The final conflict between truth and error will be over worship. This is a call to give our deepest allegiance to Christ. He is the active Agent in Creation, "for all things were made by Him." The first angel appeals to us to worship Jesus, the One who made all things.

QUESTION What two major themes summarize the three angels' messages?

Then I saw another angel flying in the midst of heaven, having the everlasting gospel to preach to those who dwell on the earth—to every nation, tribe, tongue, and people—saying with a loud voice, "Fear God and give glory to Him, for the hour of His judgment has come; and worship Him who made heaven and earth, the sea and springs of water" (Revelation 14:6, 7).

a. _____

b. _____

The three angels' messages, which proclaim the everlasting gospel and call people to worship the Creator, are at the center of earth's final conflict. The urgency of this Christ-centered message is well stated in the book *The Great Controversy*:

These truths, as presented in Revelation 14 in connection with "the everlasting gospel," will distinguish the church of Christ at the time of His appearing. For as the result of the threefold message it is announced: "Here are they that keep the commandments of God, and the faith of Jesus." And this message is the last to be given before the coming of the Lord. Immediately following its proclamation the Son of man is seen by the prophet, coming in glory to reap the harvest of the earth.[1]

God's last-day church has been given the awesome responsibility of taking the three angels' messages to the world. What a privilege God has given to His last-day church!

God's people "have been set in the world as watchmen and light bearers. To them has been entrusted the last warning for a perishing world. On them is shining wonderful light from the word of God. They have been given a work of the most solemn import—the proclamation of the first, second, and third angels' messages. There is no other work of so great importance. They are to allow nothing else to absorb their attention."[2]

God has called His church to have a clear vision of His will for them. They are called to proclaim the gospel message of the three angels in the power of the Holy Spirit to prepare the world for the soon return of Christ.

QUESTION **2** Why is this last-day conflict over worship so important? What is the basis of all true worship?

"You are worthy, O Lord,
To receive glory and honor and power;
For You created all things,
And by Your will they exist and were created" (Revelation 4:11).

The issue of worship is so crucial because it was the major issue in heaven when Lucifer, an angelic being of dazzling brightness, rebelled against God. Lucifer desired to exalt his "throne above the stars of God" (Isaiah 14:13); he wanted to rule. This angel, a created being, coveted a position higher than his Creator.

One primary reason Sabbath worship is so significant in the great controversy between good and evil is that it exalts Christ as Creator and Lord. It acknowledges His ownership of this world as Creator and the basis of all true worship. "The duty to worship God is based upon the fact that He is the Creator and that to Him all other beings owe their existence."[3]

Jesus' sign of His creative authority

QUESTION **3** When did God give the Sabbath as a sign of His creative authority?

And on the seventh day God ended His work which He had done, and He rested on the seventh day from all His work which He had done. Then God blessed the seventh day and sanctified it, because in it He rested from all His work which God had created and made.

This is the history of the heavens and the earth when they were created, in the day that the LORD God made the earth and the heavens (Genesis 2:2–4).

After the six literal days of Creation and the creation of Adam and Eve, God completed His work and established the seventh-day Sabbath as a sign of His creative authority.

"God Himself measured off the first week as a sample for successive weeks to the close of time. Like every other, it consisted of seven literal days. Six days were employed in the work of creation; upon the seventh, God rested, and He then blessed this day and set it apart as a day of rest for man."[4]

Jesus did three things on the seventh day to set it aside and mark it as the permanent memorial of His creative activity:

- *He blessed*, or infused with His divine presence, this common, ordinary twenty-four-hour period.
- *He sanctified*, or made holy, this day and by His action made it different from all other days.
- *He rested* in the completion of His work on this day. God states, "For in six days the LORD made the heavens and the earth, and on the seventh day He rested and was refreshed"

(Exodus 31:17). As we enter the Sabbath rest, we join Jesus in the refreshing rest that renews us.

Some people are still confused over which day the seventh day is. We should pause and take a few moments to confirm the identity of the seventh-day Sabbath.

Jesus, the Sabbath, and the Bible

The Bible clearly reveals which day is the seventh-day Sabbath. Luke records,

> That day was the Preparation, and the Sabbath drew near.
> And the women who had come with Him from Galilee followed after, and they observed the tomb and how His body was laid. Then they returned and prepared spices and fragrant oils. And they rested on the Sabbath according to the commandment.

Now on the first day of the week, very early in the morning, they, and certain other women with them, came to the tomb bringing the spices which they had prepared. But they found the stone rolled away from the tomb. Then they went in and did not find the body of the Lord Jesus. And it happened, as they were greatly perplexed about this, that behold, two men stood by them in shining garments. Then, as they were afraid and bowed their faces to the earth, they said to them, "Why do you seek the living among the dead? He is not here, but is risen! Remember how He spoke to you when He was still in Galilee, saying, 'The Son of Man must be delivered into the hands of sinful men, and be crucified, and the third day rise again' " (Luke 23:54–24:7).

The text is clear. Christ was

- *crucified on Friday*, the preparation day;
- *at rest on Sabbath* in the tomb; and
- *resurrected on Sunday*, the first day of the week.

This timing is significant. It not only identifies the seventh day of the week, Saturday, as the Bible Sabbath but also demonstrates that Jesus, our Example, rested on the Sabbath even in death. His closest followers followed His example and would not embalm His body until after Sabbath. Christ left them a legacy of Sabbath worship, and they followed it.

Jesus, the Sabbath, and astronomy
What about astronomy? Does it tell us whether days have been lost or the weekly cycle changed? Astronomers are unified in

their understanding regarding the continuity of the weekly cycle. Here is a statement from the United States Naval Observatory in Washington, DC: "We have had occasion to investigate the results of the works of specialists in chronology, and we have never found one of them that has ever had the slightest doubt about the continuity of the weekly cycle since long before the Christian Era."[5]

Let's take another quick look at the four significant elements of time—day, week, month, and year—in astronomy. How do we define each of them?

- Day—The day is the twenty-four hours the earth takes to rotate on its axis.
- Month—The month is the length of time the moon takes to orbit the earth.
- Year—The year is the time the earth takes to revolve around the sun—approximately 365 days.
- Week—There is *no astronomical answer* to the week. The biblical account of Creation in Genesis is the only logical answer.

Jesus, the Author and Creator of all time, has left in time an eternal memorial that enables us to worship Him as Creator.

Jesus, the Sabbath, and history
The Bible says the Sabbath was to be kept down through the ages. And God's people have kept it in all ages. Before the days of Christ and the apostles, before the Ten Commandments were given, even before Abraham fathered the Jewish people, our first parents, Adam and Eve, kept the Sabbath. Through the centuries, the Jewish people have kept an accurate record of the Sabbath. For more than four thousand years, they have kept

the true Sabbath on Saturday. Throughout history, in both Old and New Testament times, the Sabbath has been kept as an eternal sign.

Jesus, the Sabbath, and language

Here is a fascinating fact. Before the Flood that deluged the earth with water, all people spoke the same language (Genesis 11:1). Shortly after the Flood, as the population grew, in defiance of God, unconsecrated men proposed a plan to build a tower that reached up into the heavens. They thought that this would bring them security if another flood came.

At that tower, known as the Tower of Babel, God confused the languages. As a result, Genesis 11:9 records, "Therefore its name is called Babel, because there the LORD confused the languages of all the earth; and from there the LORD scattered them abroad over the face of all the earth." When God confused the languages, and as the languages continued to develop, He preserved a record of the seventh-day Sabbath in each language in honor of Jesus' creative authority. In more than one hundred languages of the world, the word for the seventh day on our calendar, called Saturday in English, is translated as *Sabbath*. There is no word for *Saturday* in these languages. The seventh day is simply called Sabbath.

There is plenty of evidence of which day is the seventh-day Sabbath from the Bible; the dictionary, astronomy, history, and languages of the world. Most important of all, Jesus kept the Sabbath and taught His disciples to keep the Sabbath. In Matthew 24:20, Jesus instructed His disciples, "And pray that your flight may not be in winter or on the Sabbath." Why would Jesus tell this to Peter, James, and John if He knew they would no longer be worshiping on that day? Jesus knew that after the Cross, they would still be worshiping on the Sabbath. So He urged them to pray that they would not have to desecrate His holy day by fleeing in panic from besieging armies.

In the last days of earth's history, as the controversy between good and evil ends, Christ will have a group of people who acknowledge His creative authority by keeping the Sabbath. Revelation 14:12 says, "Here is the patience of the saints; here are those who keep the commandments of God and the faith of Jesus."

Jesus' Creation memorial

The Sabbath was created to serve as a weekly reminder for humanity.

> "The importance of the Sabbath as the memorial of creation is that it keeps ever present the true reason why worship is due to God"—because He is the Creator, and we are His creatures. "The Sabbath therefore lies at the very foundation of divine worship, for it teaches this great truth in the most impressive manner, and no other institution does this. The true ground of divine worship, not of that on the seventh day merely, but of all worship, is found in the distinction between the Creator and His creatures. This great fact can never become obsolete, and must never be forgotten."[6]

Furthermore,

> it was to keep this truth ever before the minds of men, that God instituted the Sabbath in Eden; and so long as the fact that He is our Creator continues to be a reason why we should worship Him, so long the Sabbath will continue as its sign and memorial. Had the Sabbath been universally kept, man's

thoughts and affections would have been led to the Creator as the object of reverence and worship, and there would never have been an idolater, an atheist, or an infidel. The keeping of the Sabbath is a sign of loyalty to the true God, "Him that made heaven, and earth, and the sea, and the fountains of waters." It follows that the message which commands men to worship God and keep His commandments will especially call upon them to keep the fourth commandment.[7]

QUESTION **4** We have learned that the seventh day, Saturday, is the Bible Sabbath, but when does the Sabbath begin?

God called the light Day, and the darkness He called Night. So the evening and the morning were the first day (Genesis 1:5; see also Genesis 1:8, 13, 19, 23 and 31).

"It shall be to you a sabbath of solemn rest, and you shall afflict your souls; on the ninth day of the month at evening, from evening to evening, you shall celebrate your sabbath" (Leviticus 23:32).

The Sabbath begins on Friday evening and continues until sundown on Saturday evening. When the sun is setting on Friday evening, it is time to rest, relax, and worship the Creator. In our family, when Sabbath comes, we love to sing the song "Holy Sabbath Day of Rest":

Holy Sabbath day of rest,
By our Master richly blest,
God created and divine,
Set aside for holy time.

Yes, the holy Sabbath rest,
By our God divinely blest,
It to us a sign shall be
Throughout all eternity.

As the Sabbath draweth on,
Friday eve at set of sun,
Christian household then should meet,
Sing and pray at Jesus' feet.

Yes, the holy Sabbath rest,
By our God divinely blest,
It to us a sign shall be
Throughout all eternity.[8]

Jesus and Sabbath worship

Sabbath worship is a time of spiritual renewal. In singing, praise, giving, the preaching of the Word, and fellowship, our spiritual lives are strengthened. Sabbath is more than merely a day. Sabbath worship is an experience. The passages that follow outline that experience.

Singing and praise. Singing the message of Jesus and His redeeming love inspires us and draws us closer to Christ. Biblical, Christ-centered music touches the depths of our heart and prompts us to action. Music is God's chosen method of praise.

Serve the LORD with gladness;
Come before His presence with singing. . . .

Enter into His gates with thanksgiving,
And into His courts with praise.
Be thankful to Him, and bless His name
    (Psalm 100:2, 4).

The soul may ascend nearer heaven on the wings of praise. God is worshiped with song and music in the courts above, and as we express our gratitude we are approximating to the worship of the heavenly hosts.[9]

Our songs of praise in Sabbath worship acknowledge that Christ, our Creator, is Lord of all. As this song says,

All hail the power of Jesus' name!
Let angels prostrate fall;
Bring forth the royal diadem
And crown Him Lord of all!
Bring forth the royal diadem
And crown Him Lord of all!

Let every kindred, every tribe,
On this terrestrial ball,
To Him all majesty ascribe,
And crown Him Lord of all!
To Him all majesty ascribe,
And crown Him Lord of all![10]

Giving with a thankful heart. Giving is an act of worship that starves selfishness and acknowledges that Christ is the Creator of all things, and they belong to Him.

Give to the LORD the glory due His name;
Bring an offering, and come into His
    courts,
Oh, worship the LORD in the beauty of
    holiness! (Psalm 96:8, 9).

"Bring all the tithes into the storehouse,
That there may be food in My house,

147

And try Me now in this," says the LORD of hosts,
"If I will not open for you the windows of heaven
And pour out for you such blessing
That there will not be room enough to receive it" (Malachi 3:10).

Reading the Scriptures. As we read the Scriptures, the Holy Spirit that inspired the Word inspires our hearts.

"Men and brethren, sons of the family of Abraham, and those among you who fear God, to you the word of this salvation has been sent. For those who dwell in Jerusalem, and their rulers, because they did not know Him, nor even the voices of Prophets which are read every Sabbath, have fulfilled them in condemning Him." (Acts 13:26, 27).

"For Moses has had throughout many generations those who preach him in every city, being read in the synagogues every Sabbath" (Acts 15:21).

Praying. There is a special power in corporate, united prayer. As the congregation kneels in prayer, the Spirit of God anoints each praying heart with new spiritual strength as we draw near to Jesus.

Oh come, let us worship and bow down;
Let us kneel before the LORD our Maker.
For He is our God (Psalm 95:6, 7).

Both in public and in private worship it is our privilege to bow on our knees before God when we offer our petitions to Him. Jesus, our example, "kneeled down, and prayed." Luke 22:41. Of His disciples it is recorded that they, too, "kneeled down and prayed." Acts 9:40. . . .

True reverence for God is inspired by a sense of His infinite greatness and a realization of His presence.[11]

Preaching the Word. As we listen to a Bible-based sermon, our minds expand, and our faith grows. In addition,

To them God willed to make known what are the riches of the glory of this mystery among the Gentiles: which is Christ in you, the hope of glory. Him we preach, warning every man and teaching every man in all wisdom, that we may present every man perfect in Christ Jesus (Colossians 1:27, 28).

Paul knew that there was before the church a time of great peril. He knew that faithful, earnest work would have to be done by those left in charge of the churches; and he wrote to Timothy. "I charge thee therefore before God, and the Lord Jesus Christ, who shall judge the quick and the dead at His appearing and His kingdom; Preach the word; be instant in season, out of season; reprove, rebuke, exhort, with all long-suffering and doctrine."[12]

Fellowship. There is spiritual strength in corporate worship. Together we encourage one another on our spiritual journey. Satan hates the Sabbath because he knows that it binds God's people together in a worldwide communion of believers. This international Sabbath fellowship of worshipers from every nation, kindred, tongue, and people is a tribute of praise to our Creator, and it is a symbol of His divine supremacy. For this reason, the Sabbath will be central in the final crisis.

Jesus' seal

Revelation 7:2, 14 describes the seal of God: "Then I saw another angel ascending from the east, having the seal of the living God. . . . These are the ones who come out of the great tribulation, and washed their robes and made them white in the blood of the Lamb."

QUESTION **5** Where is God's seal contained?

Bind up the testimony,
Seal the law among my disciples (Isaiah 8:16).

In contrast to those who receive the beast's mark (Revelation 14:9), those who have God's seal worship the Creator and keep His commandments (verse 12). The commandment calling us back to worship Jesus as the Creator contains God's seal.

QUESTION **6** What specific commandment contains the characteristics of God's seal?

"Remember the Sabbath day, to keep it holy. Six days you shall labor and do all your work, but the seventh day is the Sabbath of the LORD your God. In it you shall do no work: you, nor your son, nor your daughter, nor your male servant, nor your female servant, nor your cattle, nor your stranger who is within your gates. For in six days the LORD made the heavens and the earth, the sea, and all that is in them, and rested the seventh day. Therefore, the LORD blessed the Sabbath day and hallowed it" (Exodus 20:8–11).

The fourth commandment regarding the Sabbath is the only one of all the ten where we find the name, title, and domain of the Lawgiver. Therefore, "The fourth commandment alone of all the ten contains the seal of the great Lawgiver, the Creator of the heavens and the earth."[13]

QUESTION **7** According to the Bible, what is God's special sign?

"Moreover I also gave them My Sabbaths, to be a sign between them and Me, that they might know that I am the LORD who sanctifies them" (Ezekiel 20:12).

"Hallow My Sabbaths, and they will be a sign between Me and you, that you may know that I am the LORD your God" (verse 20).

The Sabbath is a sign of God's creative power and His great love for humanity. It is the outward manifestation of an inner commitment to God in the final test over the seal of God and the mark of the beast.

QUESTION **8** How are we sealed?

And do not grieve the Holy Spirit of God, by whom you were sealed for the day of redemption (Ephesians 4:30).

The Holy Spirit solidifies our commitment to Christ. He seals us for eternity so that we will stand firm on His truth when the mark of the beast is enforced. We do not seal ourselves; the Holy Spirit seals us.

This sealing process is described by Ellen White. "Just as soon as the people of God are sealed in their foreheads—it is not any seal or mark that can be seen, but a settling into the truth, both intellectually and spiritually, so they cannot be moved—just as soon as God's people are sealed and prepared for the shaking, it will come."[14]

QUESTION 9 Where is God's seal placed?

"Do not harm the earth, the sea, or the trees till we have sealed the servants of our God on their foreheads" (Revelation 7:3).

The forehead is a symbol of the mind, the place where conscience, reason, and judgment are located. God's remnant who are sealed are totally committed to Him, and their minds and lives reflect His likeness. In truth, "the seal of the living God will be placed upon those only who bear a likeness to Christ in character."[15]

Jesus, the Sabbath, and eternity

Jesus' Sabbath worship here on earth is an example for us today and will remain so through all eternity.

QUESTION 10 Will the Sabbath be kept throughout eternity?

"And it shall come to pass
That from one New Moon to another,
And from one Sabbath to another,
All flesh shall come to worship before Me," says the LORD (Isaiah 66:23).

What a wonderful, joyous blessing it will be to worship Jesus through the endless ages of eternity. "So long as the heavens and the earth endure, the Sabbath will continue as a sign of the Creator's power. And when Eden shall bloom on earth again, God's holy rest day will be honored by all beneath the sun. 'From one Sabbath to another' the inhabitants of the glorified new earth shall go up 'to worship before Me, saith the Lord.' Matthew 5:18; Isaiah 66:23."[16]

When we worship on the Sabbath, we follow the example of Jesus and join the worship in heaven in praise and adoration to the God who made us. "All heaven is keeping the Sabbath, but not in a listless, do-nothing way. On this day every energy of the soul should be awake, for are we not to meet with God and with Christ our Saviour? We may behold Him by faith. He is longing to refresh and bless every soul."[17]

Worship is an essential part of Christian life, and Sabbath worship will become a crucial test in the last days. We receive heaven's blessing on the Sabbath when we follow Jesus' example of worship and unite with His people in praising Him.

If you would like to follow Jesus' example of worship, check the box below:

☐ Jesus, I want to follow Your example of worship. I want to come to Your sanctuary, worship You, and keep the Sabbath holy.

1. Ellen G. White, *The Great Controversy Between Christ and Satan* (Nampa, ID: Pacific Press®, 2005), 453, 454.
2. Ellen G. White, *Testimonies for the Church*, vol. 9 (Mountain View, CA: Pacific Press®, 1948), 19.
3. White, *Great Controversy*, 436.
4. Ellen G. White, *Patriarchs and Prophets* (Nampa, ID: Pacific Press®, 2005), 111.
5. U.S. Naval Observatory, James Robertson, director, letter to F. D. Nichol, March 12, 1932.
6. White, *Great Controversy*, 437, 438. Quoted material within the selection is from J. N. Andrews, *History of the Sabbath,* chapter 27.
7. White, *Great Controversy*, 438.
8. L. E. C. Joers, "Holy Sabbath, Day of Rest" (1921).
9. Ellen G. White, *Steps to Christ* (Washington, DC: Review and Herald®, 1977), 104.
10. Edward Perronet, "All Hail the Power of Jesus' Name" (1780).
11. Ellen G. White, *Prophets and Kings* (Nampa, ID: Pacific Press®, 2005), 48.
12. Ellen G. White, *The Acts of the Apostles* (Nampa, ID: Pacific Press®, 2005), 502, 503.
13. Ellen G. White, *Last Day Events* (Nampa, ID: Pacific Press®, 1992), 220.
14. White, 219, 220.
15. White, 221.
16. Ellen G. White, *The Desire of Ages* (Nampa, ID: Pacific Press®, 2005), 283.
17. Ellen G. White, *Counsels for the Church* (Nampa, ID: Pacific Press®, 1991), 267.

NOTES

LESSON 11

Jesus' Gethsemane Experience

After His three and a half years of ministry, Jesus' work on earth was coming to a close. In His great intercessory prayer in John 17, the Savior prayed, "I have glorified You on the earth. I have finished the work which You have given Me to do" (John 17:4). The entire purpose of His life was the salvation of humanity. Everything He did led to the climax of the cross. Throughout His life, He was focused on His redemptive mission—whatever the cost in physical, mental, and emotional pain. Ellen White succinctly describes His journey from the manger to Calvary in these words:

> Every pang that rent His heart, every insult that was heaped upon His head, every privation He was called to endure, was open to His view before He laid aside His crown and royal robe, and stepped down from the throne, to clothe His divinity with humanity. The path from the manger to Calvary was all before His eyes. He knew the anguish that would come upon Him. He knew it all, and yet He said, "Lo, I come: in the volume of the Book it is written of Me, I delight to do Thy will, O My God: yea, Thy law is within My heart." Psalm 40:7, 8.[1]

Jesus knew that by giving His life as a ransom, He would save the human family. His entire life was dedicated to revealing the Father's character of love. To do that, Jesus would face the agony of the second death and experience the shame and guilt that sinners will feel in their final separation from God (Galatians 3:13; Hebrews 2:9).

Gethsemane was the beginning of the end for Jesus. He left the garden to the face the farce of a trial in Pilate's judgment hall. He was interrogated in Herod's palace and flogged in a Roman courtyard before He staggered beneath the agonizing load of the cross and was crucified on a Roman stake. From Gethsemane, His pathway led to mockery, ridicule, betrayal, denial, and rejection. It led to excruciating physical pain, mental agony, and spiritual torment.

But before these final events in Christ's life, God gave Him a glimpse of glory and the assurance of His Sonship. This glimpse encouraged Him to face the dark night of suffering He was going to pass through. Before Gethsemane, Jesus experienced the Transfiguration.

Jesus' transfiguration

Matthew records, "Now after six days Jesus took Peter, James, and John his brother, led them up on a high mountain by themselves; and He was transfigured before them. His face shone like the sun, and His clothes became as white as the light" (Matthew 17:1, 2).

In answer to Jesus' prayers, Moses, who had died and was resurrected and brought to heaven, and Elijah, who had been translated without seeing death, appeared to Jesus. They assured Him that His sacrifice on the cross would be worth it. Commenting on this event, Ellen White wrote,

> The Saviour has seen the gloom of His disciples, and has longed to lighten their grief by an assurance that their faith has not been in vain. . . . Only the three who are to witness His anguish in Gethsemane have been chosen to be with Him on the mount. . . . He pleads that they may witness a manifestation of His divinity that will comfort them in the hour of His supreme agony with the knowledge that He is of a surety the Son of God and that His shameful death is a part of the plan of redemption.
>
> His prayer is heard. While He is bowed in lowliness upon the stony ground, suddenly the heavens open, the golden gates of the city of God are thrown wide, and holy radiance descends upon the mount, enshrouding the Saviour's form. Divinity from within flashes through humanity, and meets the glory coming from above. Arising from His prostrate position, Christ stands in godlike majesty. The soul agony is gone. His countenance

now shines "as the sun," and His garments are "white as the light."[2]

The disciples see Jesus is not alone. Two heavenly persons are with Him. They are Moses and Elijah. "Moses upon the mount of transfiguration was a witness to Christ's victory over sin and death. He represented those who shall come forth from the grave at the resurrection of the just. Elijah, who had been translated to heaven without seeing death, represented those who will be living upon the earth at Christ's second coming, and who will be 'changed, in a moment, in the twinkling of an eye, at the last trump;' when 'this mortal must put on immortality,' and 'this corruptible must put on incorruption.' 1 Corinthians 15:51–53."[3] Also, "while they were still gazing on the scene upon the mount, 'a bright cloud overshadowed them, and behold a voice out of the cloud, which said, "This is My beloved Son, in whom I am well pleased; hear ye Him." ' "[4]

With the assurance of the Father's love, Jesus arose to complete the work of redemption. He now knew that His death on the cross would not be in vain. Gethsemane and Golgotha were before Him, but He approached them with the glorious light of the transfiguration encouraging His heart and strengthening His spirit.

Jesus in the Garden of Gethsemane

The Garden of Gethsemane is a beautiful garden that lies at the foot of the Mount of Olives in Jerusalem. Jesus often went to Gethsemane for meditation, prayer, and rest. On the night before His crucifixion, Jesus made His way to the garden of Gethsemane with His disciples. As they came to the garden, Jesus became very quiet. He had visited the garden many times before, but the night before His crucifixion, His heart was heavy. Jesus was full of agony, weighed down with the sins of the world.

We cannot comprehend the immense sorrow and grief that Jesus bore as He entered the Garden of Gethsemane that night. Here Jesus would face the greatest trial of His life. Would He choose to go through the trial and agony of the cross and save the human race, or would He let them bear their own consequences for sin? Would He give up and go back to the Father without saving humanity? We can easily surmise that Satan tempted Him with these, or similar, thoughts:

- What would be gained by Your sacrifice?
- "The people who claim to be above all others in temporal and spiritual advantages have rejected You."[5]
- One of Your disciples will betray You—and he's not the only one who will reject Your sacrifice.
- One of Your closest disciples will deny You—they don't appreciate what You're doing for them. It's not worth it.
- All will forsake You.

Jesus' heavy burden

QUESTION **1** How heavy was the burden that rested on Jesus the night of His betrayal?

And He took with Him Peter and the two sons of Zebedee, and He began to be sorrowful and deeply distressed. Then He said to them, "My soul is exceedingly sorrowful, even to death. Stay here and watch with Me" (Matthew 26:37, 38).

The weight of the guilt of the world's sins He voluntarily accepted, and He bore the condemnation as our Sin Bearer. This weight threatened to crush out His life. As Isaiah the prophet put it, "And the LORD has laid on Him the iniquity of us all" (Isaiah 53:6).

QUESTION **2** Although Jesus was numbered among the transgressors, what was His conviction?

"And He who sent Me is with Me. The Father has not left Me alone, for I always do those things that please Him" (John 8:29).

Throughout His life and ministry, Jesus always determined to do the Father's will.

Although Jesus usually conversed with and instructed His disciples as they walked, this time, as He neared Gethsemane, He became silent. At the entrance of the garden, Jesus left all the disciples except Peter, James, and John.

These were Jesus' closest companions. Now He needed them to spend the night with Him in prayer.

QUESTION **3** What did Jesus ask His disciples to do?

Then He said to them, "My soul is exceedingly sorrowful, even to death. Stay here and watch with Me."

He went a little farther and fell on His face, and prayed, saying, "O My Father, if it is possible, let this cup pass from Me; nevertheless, not as I will, but as You will" (Matthew 26:38, 39).

Jesus asked Peter, James, and John to stay and watch with Him while He went to pray in a place nearby. Jesus knew that His most challenging hour had arrived. He knew nothing remained for Him on earth except the torture of physical pain and mental anguish.

Jesus experienced more suffering than any other human being has endured. His prayers in Gethsemane prepared Him for the trials ahead. For He would face that hour alone.

QUESTION **4** Would any of Jesus' earthly companions comfort Him in His darkest hour?

Reproach has broken my heart,
And I am full of heaviness;
I looked for someone to take pity, but there was none;
And for comforters, but I found none (Psalm 69:20).

Jesus' disciples did not comfort Him in His greatest agony. Assuredly,

the human heart longs for sympathy in suffering. This longing Christ felt to the very depths of His being. In the supreme agony of His soul He came to His disciples with a yearning desire to hear some words of comfort from those whom He had so often blessed and comforted, and shielded in sorrow and distress. The One who had always had words of sympathy for them was now suffering superhuman agony, and He longed to know that they were praying for Him and for themselves. How dark seemed the malignity of sin! Terrible was the temptation to let the

human race bear the consequences of its own guilt, while He stood innocent before God. If He could only know that His disciples understood and appreciated this, He would be strengthened.[6]

QUESTION 5 When Jesus approached the disciples, what did He ask Peter?

Then He came to the disciples and found them sleeping, and said to Peter, "What! Could you not watch with Me one hour?" (Matthew 26:40).

Though Jesus asked them to watch and pray, the disciples fell asleep. "To 'watch' means, literally, 'to stay awake,' but here it means to remain awake for a purpose, and that purpose is to share Christ's vigil."[7] In truth, "the disciples trusted to themselves. They did not look to the mighty Helper as Christ had counseled them to do. Thus when the Saviour was most in need of their sympathy and prayers, they were found asleep. Even Peter was sleeping."[8]

Jesus' victory over Satan in Gethsemane
Satan knew this was his last attempt to have Jesus give up on the salvation of the human race.

Now the tempter had come for the last fearful struggle. For this he had been preparing during the three years of Christ's ministry. Everything was at stake with him. If he failed here, his hope of mastery was lost; the kingdoms of the world would finally become Christ's; he himself would be overthrown and cast out. But if Christ could be overcome, the earth would become Satan's kingdom, and the human race would be forever in his power. With the issues of the conflict before Him, Christ's soul was filled with dread of separation from God. Satan told Him that if He became the surety for a sinful world, the separation would be eternal. He would be identified with Satan's kingdom, and would nevermore be one with God.[9]

Jesus' physical form in the Garden of Gethsemane

QUESTION **6** When the disciples awakened from their slumber, and they saw Jesus, what did Jesus' physical form look like?

Just as many were astonished at you,
So His visage was marred more than any man,
And His form more than the sons of men (Isaiah 52:14).

When Jesus came to check on His disciples and gather encouragement from them, He found them asleep. Nevertheless,

the disciples awakened at the voice of Jesus, but they hardly knew Him, His face was so changed by anguish. Addressing Peter, Jesus said, "Simon, sleepest thou? couldest not thou watch one hour? Watch ye and pray, lest ye enter into temptation. The spirit truly is ready, but the flesh is weak." The weakness of His disciples awakened the sympathy of Jesus. He feared that they would not be able to endure the test which would come upon them in His betrayal and death. He did not reprove them, but said, "Watch ye and pray, lest ye enter into temptation." Even in His great agony, He was seeking to excuse their weakness.[10]

QUESTION **7** What request did Jesus make to the Father three times that showed the redemption of a lost world trembled in the balance?

He went a little farther and fell on His face, and prayed, saying, "O My Father, if it is possible, let this cup pass from Me; nevertheless, not as I will, but as You will" (Matthew 26:39).

160

"O My Father, if this cup cannot pass away from Me unless I drink it, Your will be done" (verse 42).

As He prayed in Gethsemane, Jesus asked the Father to take away the cup that was before Him.

Three times has He uttered that prayer. Three times has humanity shrunk from the last, crowning sacrifice. But now the history of the human race comes up before the world's Redeemer. He sees that the transgressors of the law, if left to themselves, must perish. He sees the helplessness of man. He sees the power of sin. The woes and lamentations of a doomed world rise before Him. He beholds its impending fate, and His decision is made. He will save man at any cost to Himself. He accepts His baptism of blood, that through Him perishing millions may gain everlasting life. He has left the courts of heaven, where all is purity, happiness, and glory, to save the one lost sheep, the one world that has fallen by transgression. And He will not turn from His mission. He will become the propitiation of a race that has willed to sin. His prayer now breathes only submission: "If this cup may not pass away from Me, except I drink it, Thy will be done."[11]

Every one of us sometime in our lives will experience the cup of suffering. We can have one of three reactions to this cup:

❶ We can reject the cup by refusing to accept what has happened and become angry at God over giving us the cup.

❷ We can receive the cup with resentment and exclaim, "Thy will be done," with the resignation of defeat and become discouraged.

❸ We can receive the cup with the assurance that God will not allow us to be tempted above what we can bear (1 Corinthians 10:13). We can say with Christ, "Thy will be done" with the absolute certainty that God will provide strength for our journey.

Jesus suffered alone

Isaiah the prophet predicted that Jesus would have to go through the Gethsemane experience alone.

"I have trodden the winepress alone,
And from the peoples no one was with Me.
For I have trodden them in My anger,
And trampled them in My fury;
Their blood is sprinkled upon My garments,
And I have stained all My robes" (Isaiah 63:3).

Sin is so offensive to God that Jesus had to suffer the horrible ordeal of Gethsemane alone. In truth,

The Saviour trod the wine press alone, and of the people there was none with Him.

But God suffered with His Son. Angels beheld the Saviour's agony. They saw their Lord enclosed by legions of satanic forces, His nature weighed down with a shuddering, mysterious dread. There was silence in heaven. No harp was touched. Could mortals have viewed the amazement of the angelic host as in silent grief they watched the Father separating His beams of light, love, and glory from His beloved Son, they would better understand how offensive in His sight is sin.[12]

Furthermore,

the worlds unfallen and the heavenly angels had watched with intense interest as the conflict drew to its close. Satan and his confederacy of evil, the legions of apostasy, watched intently this great crisis in the work of redemption. The powers of good and evil waited to see what answer would come to Christ's thrice-repeated prayer. Angels had longed to bring relief to the divine sufferer, but this might not be. No way of escape was found for the Son of God. In this awful crisis, when everything was at stake, when the mysterious cup trembled in the hand of the sufferer, the heavens opened, a light shone forth amid the stormy darkness of the crisis hour, and the mighty angel who stands in God's presence, occupying the position from which Satan fell, came to the side of Christ.[13]

Jesus and the angel Gabriel

When Jesus finished praying, God sent the angel Gabriel to minister to Him. However,

the angel came not to take the cup

from Christ's hand, but to strengthen Him to drink it, with the assurance of the Father's love. He came to give power to the divine-human suppliant. He pointed Him to the open heavens, telling Him of the souls that would be saved as the result of His sufferings. He assured Him that His Father is greater and more powerful than Satan, that His death would result in the utter discomfiture of Satan, and that the kingdom of this world would be given to the saints of the Most High. He told Him that He would see of the travail of His soul, and be satisfied, for He would see a multitude of the human race saved, eternally saved.[14]

QUESTION **8** How great were Jesus' suffering and agony in the garden that night?

And being in agony, He prayed more earnestly. Then His sweat became like great drops of blood falling down to the ground (Luke 22:44).

Jesus suffered intensely in Gethsemane, "Again, the Son of God was seized with super-human agony, and fainting and exhausted, He staggered back to the place of His former struggle. His suffering was even greater than before. As the agony of soul came upon Him, 'His sweat was as it were great drops of blood falling down to the ground.' "[15]

Jesus prays for the Father to take away His agony

QUESTION **9** After Jesus prayed three times for the Father to take away the cup of agony, what happened next?

Then He came to His disciples and said to them, "Are you still sleeping and resting? Behold, the hour is at hand, and the Son of Man is being betrayed into the hands of sinners. Rise, let us be going. See, My betrayer is at hand" (Matthew 26:45, 46).

Jesus' hour had come. As Jesus rejoined His disciples,

no traces of His recent agony were visible as Jesus stepped forth to meet His betrayer. Standing in advance of His disciples He said, "Whom seek ye?" They answered, "Jesus of Nazareth." Jesus replied, "I am He." As these words were spoken, the angel who had lately ministered to Jesus moved between Him and the mob. A divine light illuminated the Saviour's face, and a dovelike form overshadowed Him. In the presence of this divine glory, the murderous throng could not stand for a moment. They staggered back. Priests, elders, soldiers, and even Judas, fell as dead men to the ground.

The angel withdrew, and the light faded away. Jesus had opportunity to escape, but He remained, calm and self-possessed. As one glorified He stood in the midst of that hardened band, now prostrate and helpless at His feet. The disciples looked on, silent with wonder and awe.[16]

Jesus stepped forward with confidence to meet His betrayer and the mob that came to arrest Him. Judas greeted Him with a kiss—to indicate to the mob that He was Jesus of Nazareth. This was done to fulfill the Scriptures. The psalmist wrote, "Even my own familiar friend in whom I trusted, who ate my bread, has lifted up his heel against me" (Psalm 41:9). The Almighty Savior, the King of kings, the Creator of the universe, was now led away to the home of the high priest.

What Jesus had to experience next is incomprehensible, but He would not be deterred from the plan of salvation. His heart's desire was to please God. He loves us so much, He wants us to be with Him throughout eternity. The desire of every born-again Christian who has been transformed by God's grace also is to do the Father's will.

I want to understand what Jesus went through and accept His sacrifice on my behalf so that I can be saved and live eternally with Him. If you desire to allow Jesus into your heart completely and for Him to change your life, please check the box below.

☐ I choose to allow Jesus into my heart to completely change my nature.

1. Ellen G. White, *The Desire of Ages* (Nampa, ID: Pacific Press®, 2005), 410.
2. White, 420, 421.
3. White, 421, 422.
4. White, 425.
5. White, 687.
6. White, 687, 688.
7. Francis D. Nichol, ed., *Seventh-day Adventist Bible Commentary*, vol. 5 of the Commentary Reference Series (Washington, DC: Review and Herald®, 1980), 525.
8. White, *Desire of Ages*, 688, 689.
9. White, 686, 687.
10. White, 689.
11. White, 690, 693.
12. White, 693.
13. White, 693.
14. White, 693, 694.
15. White, 689.
16. White, 694.

NOTES

LESSON 12

Jesus' Betrayal and Trial

In our last lesson, we studied Jesus' trying ordeal in Gethsemane. His end was near, and in response to His heartfelt, earnest prayers, angels of God strengthened Him for the trial ahead. Satan tried to tempt Jesus to give up, and then the whole plan of redemption would fail. Our salvation weighed in the balance. Let's take another brief look at Jesus in Gethsemane. We will discover the source of His strength to face the events that would soon unfold. Jesus longed for someone to understand the enormity of the ordeal He was going through.

Jesus in the Garden of Gethsemane

Jesus feared that in His human condition, He would not be able to endure the coming conflict. However, He knew that His Father would never leave Him. His earlier statements of the Father's presence gave Him renewed assurance. "He who sent Me is with Me. The Father has not left Me alone, for I always do those things that please Him" (John 8:29). He lived a life of trust. Three times in Gethsemane, He prayed, "Thy will be done." He arose to face the challenges with confidence that His Father would sustain Him in the days ahead.

In the quiet place of prayer, He received strength to meet the injustice, rejection, and cruelty that was coming.

A heavenly peace rested upon His bloodstained face. He had borne that which no human being could ever bear; for He had tasted the sufferings of death for every man.

The sleeping disciples had been suddenly awakened by the light surrounding the Saviour. They saw the angel bending over their prostrate Master. They saw him lift the Saviour's head upon his bosom, and point toward heaven. They heard his voice, like sweetest music, speaking words of comfort and hope.[1]

Jesus' betrayer

Jesus' hour had come. His death was near. Judas, one of His own disciples would betray Him. The deepest pain comes when someone we have known and loved betrays us. Jesus' heartache was magnified because He loved Judas so deeply.

Then He came to His disciples and said to them, "Are you still sleeping and resting? Behold, the hour is at hand, and the Son of Man is being betrayed into the hands of sinners. Rise, let us be going. See, My betrayer is at hand."

And while He was still speaking, behold, Judas, one of the twelve, with a great multitude with swords and clubs, came from the chief priests and elders of the people.

Now His betrayer had given them a sign, saying, "Whomever I kiss, He is the One; seize Him." Immediately he went up to Jesus and said, "Greetings, Rabbi!" and kissed Him.

But Jesus said to him, "Friend, why have you come?"

Then they came and laid hands on Jesus and took Him (Matthew 26:45–50).

John 18:1–7 also describes the initial encounter between Jesus and the mob.

Jesus therefore, knowing all things that would come upon Him, went forward and said to them, "Whom are you seeking?"

They answered Him, "Jesus of Nazareth."

Jesus said to them, "I am He." . . . Now when He said to them, "I am He," they drew back and fell to the ground (verses 4–6).

The angel who had ministered to Jesus stepped between Him and the mob, knocking the crowd to the ground. Ellen White describes this meeting: "The angel withdrew, and the light faded away. Jesus had the opportunity to escape, but He remained, calm and self-possessed. As one glorified He stood in the midst of that hardened band, now prostrate and helpless at His feet. The disciples looked on, silent with wonder and awe."[2]

Then the scene changed. The mob got up and gathered around Jesus. Judas, the betrayer, led the mob. "The Roman soldiers, the priests and Judas, gathered about Christ. They seemed ashamed of their weakness, and fearful that He would yet escape. Again the question was asked by the Redeemer, 'Whom seek ye?' They had had evidence that He who stood before them was the Son of God, but they would not be convinced."[3] Judas knew well what he had to do. Although Judas had followed Jesus throughout His ministry,

now he [Judas] pretends to have no part with them. Coming close to Jesus, he takes His hand as a familiar friend. With the words, "Hail, Master," he kisses Him repeatedly, and appears to weep as if in sympathy with Him in His peril. . . .

The mob grew bold as they saw Judas touch the person of Him who had so recently been glorified before their eyes. They now laid hold of Jesus, and proceeded to bind those precious hands that had ever been employed in doing good.[4]

The disciples were amazed that Jesus would permit Himself to be taken by the angry mob. They could not understand what He was doing. At this point, the disciples decided that they should save themselves and fled from Jesus' presence. They all forsook Him—just as Jesus had said earlier: "Indeed the hour is coming, yes, has now come, that you will be scattered, each to his own, and will leave Me alone. And yet I am not alone, because the Father is with Me" (John 16:32).

The question can be logically asked, how could Judas ever betray Jesus? What motivated him to betray His Master? He had lived with Jesus for three and a half years. Judas had watched Jesus open blind eyes and unstop deaf ears and heal withered limbs. He listened to Jesus' powerful, life-changing sermons. Judas watched as Jesus broke the bread and fed five thousand on the hillside of Galilee. He was in the boat when Jesus calmed the storm and stilled the waters of the sea. How could Judas possibly betray Jesus? There is a simple answer: selfishness. Judas had cherished pride, greed, and love for self in his heart. As treasurer of the disciples, he began taking small amounts of money from the little the disciples had received from grateful people.

This cancer of selfishness grew until he wanted to force Jesus to declare His power and become the ruler in Israel. If this happened, self-centered Judas thought he would have a prominent place in Christ's new kingdom.

One sin cherished, one evil trait nurtured, one rebellious attitude unforsaken, leads to betrayal and eventually eternal death. Judas' fate should speak to each of us of the need for total surrender to Christ.

Jesus before the court of Caiaphas

The unruly mob—hardened Jewish leaders and rugged Roman soldiers—rushed Jesus along the rocky path, across the Kidron Valley, and up the winding dirt path to Jerusalem. As they went, Jesus' godlike appearance impressed even the most hardened in the crowd. Something about Him was different.

QUESTION **1** Where did the mob take Jesus after they seized Him?

Having arrested Him, they led Him and brought Him into the high priest's house. But Peter followed at a distance (Luke 22:54).

And those who had laid hold of Jesus led Him away to Caiaphas the high priest, where the scribes and the elders were assembled (Matthew 26:57).

_____

_____

Luke provides us with divine insight when he says "Peter followed at a distance." Following Jesus at a distance is always dangerous. It precedes denying Him. In Pilate's courtyard, Jesus was subject to mocking and ridicule. It is almost incomprehensible that the Son of God, the Creator of the universe, was subject to such cruel abuse, tortured like a common criminal. Describing the scene, Luke records, "Now the men who held Jesus mocked Him and beat Him. And having blindfolded Him, they struck Him on the face and asked Him, saying, 'Prophesy! Who is the one who struck You?' And many other things they blasphemously spoke against Him" (Luke 22:63–65).

Who is this Jesus who suffers so? He is the divine Son of God, the One who created all things. The One who is worshiped by millions of angels. Now His disciples forsook Him. Judas betrayed Him; Peter denied Him; the Jews mocked and ridiculed Him. Who is this amazing, awesome, wonderful Jesus? He is the Messiah. The One who lives from everlasting to everlasting.

QUESTION **2** While Jesus was at the high priest's house, what was Peter's reaction to Christ's sufferings?

And a certain servant girl, seeing him [Peter] as he sat by the fire, looked intently at him and said, "This man was also with Him."

But he denied Him, saying, "Woman, I do not know Him."

And after a little while another saw him and said, "You also are of them."

But Peter said, "Man, I am not!"

Then after about an hour had passed, another confidently affirmed, saying, "Surely this fellow also was with Him, for he is a Galilean."

But Peter said, "Man, I do not know what you are saying!"

Immediately, while he was still speaking, the rooster crowed. And the Lord turned and looked at Peter. Then Peter remembered the word of the Lord, how He had said to him, "Before the rooster crows, you will deny Me three times." So Peter went out and wept bitterly (Luke 22:56–62).

Peter's self-confidence, his assurance that he would never deny Christ, led him to trust in his own strength and fail Christ in His time of greatest need.

Jesus faces the Sanhedrin

After the mock trial at the high priest's house, the mob ushered Jesus to a trial in front of the Sanhedrin:

> As soon as it was day, the elders of the people, both chief priests and scribes, came together and led Him into their council, saying, "If You are the Christ, tell us."
>
> But He said to them, "If I tell you, you will by no means believe. And if I also ask you, you will by no means answer Me or let Me go. Hereafter the Son of Man will sit on the right hand of the power of God."
>
> Then they all said, "Are You then the Son of God?"
>
> So He said to them, "You rightly say that I am."
>
> And they said, "What further testimony do we need? For we have heard it ourselves from His own mouth" (Luke 22:66–71).

The religious leaders thought they were judging Jesus, but they were the ones facing judgment. They were on trial, and all heaven witnessed their rejection and rebellion.

QUESTION **3** When Jesus faced the elders, chief priests, and scribes in the Sanhedrin, what was their basis for condemning Him?

> Then they all said, "Are You then the Son of God?"
> So He said to them, "You rightly say that I am."
> And they said, "What further testimony do we need? For we have heard it ourselves from His own mouth" (Luke 22:70, 71).

_____

_____

Jesus before Pilate

These leaders in Israel chose to embrace their mistaken understanding of Scripture and timeworn traditions rather than walk in the light of the truth that Heaven revealed. Jesus was brought to the religious leaders, then to Pilate and Herod, and then back to Pilate. In the providence of God, in Jesus' darkest moments, He witnessed to eternal truths in the highest religious and political chambers in the nation.

The saga of Pilate's repeated compromises provides important lessons for our spiritual lives. The description found in Luke's account of Pilate's actions powerfully reveals the pitfalls of compromise. The more the Roman ruler compromised, the more he became shackled with chains he could not break.

Pilate's first compromise. Luke records the scene in these words:

> Then the whole multitude of them arose and led Him to Pilate. And they began to accuse Him, saying,

"We found this fellow perverting the nation, and forbidding to pay taxes to Caesar, saying that He Himself is Christ, a King."

Then Pilate asked Him, saying, "Are You the King of the Jews?"

He answered him and said, "It is as you say."

So Pilate said to the chief priests and the crowd, "I find no fault in this Man" (Luke 23:1–4).

Commenting on this scene, Ellen White wrote, "Pilate looked at the men who had Jesus in charge, and then his gaze rested searchingly on Jesus. He had had to deal with all kinds of criminals; but never before had a man bearing marks of such goodness and nobility been brought before him. On his face he saw no sign of guilt, no expression of fear, no boldness or defiance. He saw a man of calm and dignified bearing, whose countenance bore not the marks of a criminal, but the signature of heaven."[5]

Furthermore, "Christ's appearance made a favorable impression upon Pilate. His better nature was roused. He had heard of Jesus and His works. His wife had told him something of the wonderful deeds performed by the Galilean prophet, who cured the sick and raised the dead. Now this revived as a dream in Pilate's mind. He recalled rumors that he had heard from several sources. He resolved to demand of the Jews their charges against the prisoner."[6]

There are two noteworthy facts here.

First, God always sends a message to warn people of the dangers they face in compromise. This warning may come

- through the conviction of the Holy Spirit,
- through reading the Word of God,
- through some providence of God, or
- through another individual.

The second lesson is that when God impresses you to do something, do it. Why would Pilate send Jesus to Herod when he declared that he "found no fault in Jesus"? If there was no fault in Him, the logical thing to do was to let Him go free. But this was not the last Pilate would see of Jesus.

QUESTION **4** When Jesus was sent to Herod, what did Herod do?

Then Herod, with his men of war, treated Him with contempt and mocked Him, arrayed Him in a gorgeous robe, and sent Him back to Pilate (Luke 23:11).

_____

_____

Luke recorded how the scene played out in Herod's judgment hall. "Now when Herod saw Jesus, he was exceedingly glad; for he had desired for a long time to see Him, because he had heard many things about Him, and he hoped to see some miracle done by Him. Then he questioned Him with many words, but He answered him nothing. And the chief priests and scribes stood and vehemently accused Him" (Luke 23:8–10).

Herod demanded that Jesus perform a miracle. "Herod promised that if Christ would perform some miracle in his presence, He should be released. Christ's accusers had seen with their own eyes the mighty works wrought by His power. . . . Fear seized them lest He should now work a miracle. Of all things they most dreaded an exhibition of His power. Such a manifestation would prove a deathblow to their plans, and would perhaps cost them their lives."[7] Although Herod had hardened his heart, he would not condemn Jesus. He wished to relieve himself of this terrible responsibility, and so he sent Him back to Pilate.

God had a divine strategy, even in Christ's appearance before Herod. Jesus' divine appearance, even while suffering, impressed those in the royal court. The Holy Spirit impressed hearts with eternal truths. Christ's death on the cross would be for all people—even those who played a part in putting Him to death.

Pilate's second compromise. Pilate was very disappointed when the accusers brought Jesus back to him. Pilate reminded them that he had already examined Jesus and found no fault in Him. He told them that they had not proved any of the charges against Him. Herod's response to the Jewish leaders had been similar. After examining Jesus, he, too, acknowledged that Jesus had done nothing worthy of any criminal charges.

QUESTION **5** How did Pilate handle this second encounter with Christ? What did he do?

Then Pilate, when he had called together the chief priests, the rulers, and the people, said to them, "You have brought this Man to me, as one who misleads the people. And indeed, having examined Him in your presence, I have found no fault in this Man concerning those things of which you accuse Him; no, neither did Herod, for I sent you back to him; and indeed nothing deserving of death has been done by Him. I will therefore chastise Him and release Him" (for it was necessary for him to release one to them at the feast) (Luke 23:13–17).

Pilate ventured further onto the devil's ground. The crowd wanted blood, and Pilate chose to give them what they wanted, hoping to satisfy them before letting Jesus go. As he plunged further into compromise, the crowd sensed his weakness and clamored for more. Pilate's indecision and compromise only hardened their position even more. They would not stop until they had what they wanted, the crucifixion and death of Jesus. After having Jesus scourged, Pilate thought of a brilliant idea—or so he thought.

Pilate's third compromise. It was a Roman custom on a major Jewish feast to offer to free a Jewish prisoner. Pilate chose one of the vilest, most vicious criminals, named Barabbas. He then made an offer to the screaming mob. He asked them if they wanted him to release Jesus or Barabbas. Their response was shocking. It demonstrated how far Satan's forces would go to destroy Christ.

QUESTION **6** What was the crowd's response to Pilate's offer to free either Barabbas or Jesus? Why do you think they choose a hardened criminal over the Son of God?

And they all cried out at once, saying, "Away with this Man, and release to us Barabbas"—who had been thrown into prison for a certain rebellion made in the city, and for murder (Luke 23:18, 19).

Jesus gave Pilate every opportunity to know for himself the fact that He was the Messiah. "Hoping to gain the truth from Him and to escape the tumult of the crowd, Pilate took Jesus aside with him, and again questioned, 'Art Thou the King of the Jews?' "[8] The Holy Spirit was working on Pilate's heart. Conviction deepened in his soul, but he would not surrender to the moving of the Holy Spirit. He steeled himself against the divine impressions. "Jesus did not directly answer [Pilate's] question. He knew that the Holy Spirit was striving with Pilate, and He gave him opportunity to acknowledge his conviction. 'Sayest thou this thing of thyself,' He asked, 'or did others tell it thee of Me?' "[9]

Unfortunately, because of his persistent delay and compromise,

Pilate's golden opportunity had passed. Yet Jesus did not leave him without further light. While He did not directly answer Pilate's question, He plainly stated His own mission. He gave Pilate to understand that He was not seeking an earthly throne.

"My kingdom is not of this world," He said. . . .

Pilate had a desire to know the truth. His mind was confused. He eagerly grasped the words of the Saviour, and his heart was stirred with a great longing to know what it really was, and how he could obtain it.[10]

Disregarding the conviction pressing on his heart, Pilate vacillated on his final judgment. Then,

while Pilate was hesitating as to what he should do, a messenger pressed through the crowd, and handed him the letter from his wife, which read:

"Have thou nothing to do with that just Man: for I have suffered many things this day in a dream because of Him."[11]

Moreover,

Pilate's face grew pale. He was confused by his own conflicting emotions. But while he had been delaying to act, the priests and rulers were still further inflaming the minds of the people. Pilate was forced to action. He now bethought himself of a custom which might serve to secure Christ's release. It was customary at this feast to release some one prisoner

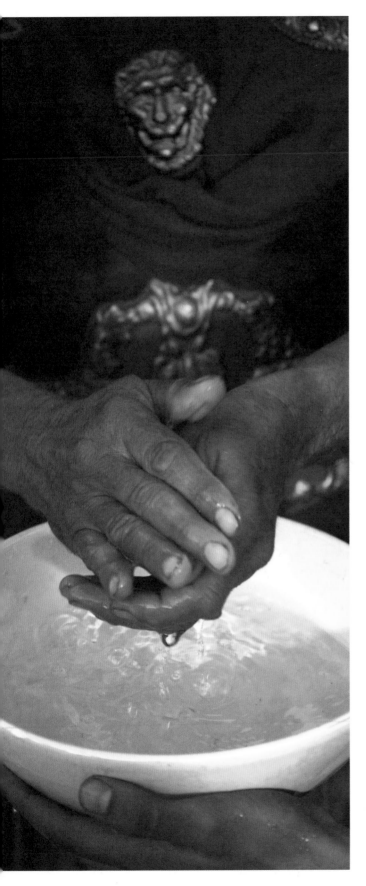

whom the people might choose. . . . The Roman authorities at this time held a prisoner named Barabbas, who was under sentence of death. This man claimed to be the Messiah. He claimed authority to establish a different order of things, to set the world right.[12]

Pilate thought to arouse the crowd to a sense of justice. He hoped to gain their sympathy for Jesus in opposition to the priests and rulers. So, turning to the crowd, he said with great earnestness, "Whom will ye that I release unto you? Barabbas, or Jesus which is called Christ?"[13]

Luke describes the scene,

Pilate, therefore, wishing to release Jesus, again called out to them. But they shouted, saying, "Crucify Him, crucify Him!"

Then he said to them the third time, "Why, what evil has He done? I have found no reason for death in Him. I will therefore chastise Him and let Him go."

But they were insistent, demanding with loud voices that He be crucified. And the voices of these men and of the chief priests prevailed. So Pilate gave sentence that it should be as they requested. And he released to them the one they requested, who for rebellion and murder had been thrown into prison; but he delivered Jesus to their will (Luke 22:20–25).

Pilate was surprised that the crowd chose Barabbas, an obvious criminal, over Jesus. The latter had done much good through His teachings and miracles. When, in a futile attempt to rid himself of any blame, Pilate washed his hands, declaring "himself innocent of the blood of Christ, Caiaphas answered defiantly, 'His blood be on us, and on our children.' "[14]

The Roman and Jewish leaders had made their final, irrevocable decision. They sealed their eternal doom. The One they judged was rendering final judgment upon them.

When Christ shall come to the earth again, not as a prisoner surrounded by a rabble will men see Him. They will see Him then as heaven's King. Christ will come in His own glory, in the glory of His Father, and the glory of the holy angels. Ten thousand times ten thousand, and thousands of thousands of angels, the beautiful and triumphant sons of God, possessing surpassing loveliness and glory, will escort Him on His way. Then shall He sit upon the throne of His glory, and before Him shall be gathered all nations. Then every eye shall see Him, and they also that pierced Him. In the place of a crown of thorns, He will wear a crown of glory,—a crown within a crown. In place of that old purple kingly robe, He will be clothed in raiment of whitest white, "so as no fuller on earth can white them." Mark 9:3. And on His vesture and on His thigh a name will be written, "King of kings, and Lord of lords." Revelation 19:16.[15]

Every one of us will be faced with the decision of the crowd that day—Jesus or Barabbas. Two choices lie before us: Christ or Satan, truth or falsehood, heaven or hell, the temporary alluring pleasures of this world or the enduring treasures of eternity.

God is doing everything He can to lead us to make eternal choices, and the devil is doing everything he can to keep us from making those choices. In this critical hour of human history, the choice is ours. Will you choose to make a complete surrender to Jesus now? If so, check the box below:

☐ I do not want to compromise my faith in Jesus. I want to allow Jesus into my heart to completely change my life.

In our next lesson, we will discover what Jesus went through at Calvary.

---

1. Ellen G. White, *The Desire of Ages* (Nampa, ID: Pacific Press®, 2005), 694.
2. White, 694.
3. White, 695.
4. White, 695, 696.
5. White, 724.
6. White, 724.
7. White, 729, 730.
8. White, 726.
9. White, 726, 727.
10. White, 727.
11. White, 732.
12. White, 733.
13. White, 733.
14. White, 738.
15. White, 739.

NOTES

LESSON 13

Jesus' Death at Calvary

God's love revealed in Christ's death on the cross has captured the attention of people from all walks of life for the last two thousand years. There is a magnetic attraction about the cross—a fascination that draws people. Hollywood produces feature films about it. Popular musicians sing about it. Authors write about it. Poets refer to it. Preachers preach about it. Why? What is so attractive about a man dying on a cross? Crucifixion was a commonly used Roman method of capital punishment. Thousands of people were slaughtered this way in the first century. What is so special about Christ's death? Countless martyrs have died for righteous causes. But there is something distinctly different about God dwelling in human flesh and voluntarily sacrificing His life on a Roman cross.

Jesus said, "And I, if I am lifted up from the earth, will draw all peoples to Myself" (John 12:32). In this lesson, we will explore the deep spiritual meaning of the cross. We will plumb its depths and discover why it has changed the lives of millions of people through the ages. We will journey with Christ from Pilate's judgment hall to Calvary.

Jesus in Pilate's judgment hall

Many in the crowd that gathered in Pilate's courtyard for the trial of Christ were among those who previously cried "Hosanna" and waved palm branches as He rode triumphantly into Jerusalem. But now, influenced by the Jewish religious leaders, when given a choice, they chose the criminal Barabbas rather than Christ. In response to Pilate's question,

"What then shall I do with Jesus who is called Christ?"

They all said to him, "Let Him be crucified!"

Then the governor said, "Why, what evil has He done?"

But they cried out all the more, saying, "Let Him be crucified!"

When Pilate saw that he could not prevail at all, but rather that a tumult was rising, he took water and washed his hands before the multitude, saying, "I am innocent of the blood of this just Person. You see to it" (Matthew 27:22–26).

Pilate's continual compromise placed him in a position where he was willing to put to death an innocent man rather than incur the hostility of an angry crowd. He yielded to their insistent pleading as they shouted, "Crucify Him, crucify Him!" He released Barabbas, had Jesus scourged, and delivered Him to be crucified. According to verses 27–31, the Roman soldiers treated the Son of God harshly: They stripped Him to the waist and put a scarlet robe on Him. They twisted a crown of thorns, put it on His head, and placed a reed in His right hand. Then they bowed before Him and mocked Him, saying, "Hail, King of the Jews!" They then led Him away to be crucified.

After the scourging, the cross that had been prepared for Barabbas was now thrust upon Jesus' bruised and bleeding body. He slowly made His way over the cobblestone streets of Jerusalem. Each step brought intense pain. News of Christ's crucifixion spread rapidly through Jerusalem. It was the Passover, and the city was packed with thousands of worshipers from places throughout the empire. The streets were full of people. Roman soldiers forced Christ through the crowded roadway to the place of execution. Weakened by the loss of blood from being scourged, famished from a lack of nourishment, and totally exhausted, He stumbled and fell beneath the heavy load. The crowd that followed Jesus saw His weak condition.

Some looked on with pity, but others with hardened hearts had no compassion. They mocked and reviled Jesus because He was unable to carry the cross. When the Roman soldiers saw that Jesus couldn't continue, they picked one man out of the crowd to assist Jesus. Simon was a Cyrenian from northern Africa who looked with compassion on Christ. They compelled him to carry the cross.

QUESTION 1 What prophecy did Isaiah make about Christ that supported Him on His journey to Golgotha?

"I have trodden the winepress alone,
And from the peoples no one was with Me.
For I have trodden them in My anger,
And trampled them in My fury;
Their blood is sprinkled upon My garments,
And I have stained all My robes" (Isaiah 63:3).

Commenting further on Jesus' walk to Calvary, Ellen White wrote, "The Saviour made no murmur of complaint. His face remained calm and serene, but great drops of sweat stood upon His brow. There was no pitying hand to wipe the death dew from His face, nor words of sympathy and unchanging fidelity to stay His human heart."[1]

Mary, the mother of Jesus, watched as her Son made His way to Calvary. "She had seen Him fainting under the burden of the cross, and had longed to place a supporting hand beneath His wounded head, and to bathe that brow which had once been pillowed upon her bosom. But she was not permitted this mournful privilege."[2]

Jesus' prayer for His enemies included you and me

QUESTION **2** While hanging on the cross, what prayer did Jesus offer for the Roman soldiers who were doing their terrible work that day?

Then Jesus said, "Father, forgive them, for they do not know what they do" (Luke 23:34).

Though He was suffering excruciating pain, Jesus' thoughts were focused on completing His mission to save sinners. "While the soldiers were doing their fearful work, Jesus prayed for His enemies, 'Father, forgive them; for they know not what they do.' His mind passed from His own suffering to the sin of His persecutors, and the terrible retribution that would be theirs. No curses were called down upon the soldiers who were handling Him so roughly. No vengeance was invoked upon the priests and rulers, who were gloating over the accomplishment of their purpose. Christ pitied them in their ignorance and guilt."[3]

Furthermore, "that prayer of Christ for His enemies embraced the world. It took in every sinner that had lived or should live, from the beginning of the world to the end of time. Upon all rests the guilt of crucifying the Son of God. To all, forgiveness is freely offered. 'Whosoever will' may have peace with God, and inherit eternal life."[4] This prayer is significant. It "embraced the world." It was not merely for the Roman soldiers who crucified Jesus. We daily crucify Him again with our sins. His forgiveness is for us. His mercy is for us. His grace is for us.

Even as Jesus prayed, the soldiers nailed Him to the cross. Then, "as soon as Jesus was nailed to the cross, it was lifted by strong men, and with great violence thrust into the place prepared for it. This caused the most intense agony to the Son of God."[5]

Jesus, the King of the Jews

Frequently, the reason for the death sentence was posted over the person being crucified. In Jesus' case, Pilate ordered that a sign be written in Hebrew, Greek, and Latin and hung on Jesus' cross (John 19:20). The sign read, "Jesus of Nazareth, the King of the Jews" (verse 19). *The Desire of Ages* sheds further light on the scene:

The priests saw what they had done, and asked Pilate to change the inscription. They said, "Write not, The King of the Jews; but that He said, I am King of the Jews." But Pilate was angry with himself because of his former weakness, and he thoroughly despised the jealous and artful priests and rulers. He replied coldly, "What I have written I have written."

A higher power than Pilate or the Jews had directed the placing of that inscription above the head of Jesus. In the providence of God, it was to awaken thought, and investigation of the Scriptures. The place where Christ was crucified was near to the

181

city. Thousands of people from all lands were then at Jerusalem, and the inscription declaring Jesus of Nazareth the Messiah would come to their notice. It was a living truth, transcribed by a hand that God had guided.[6]

Those who were passing by mocked Jesus while He was on the cross saying, "You who destroy the temple and build it in three days, save Yourself! If You are the Son of God, come down from the cross. . . . He saved others; Himself He cannot save. If He is the King of Israel, let Him now come down from the cross, and we will believe Him. He trusted in God; let Him deliver Him now if He will have Him; for He said, 'I am the Son of God' " (Matthew 27:40, 42, 43). The act suggested in the jeering cry "If You are the Son of God, come down from the cross" could have been completed by Jesus that day. However, if Jesus had chosen to come down from the cross, we would all be lost eternally. We may well ask:

- Who is this who is mocked and dying?
- Who is this who has nails through His hands?
- Who is this who has blood running down His face?
- Who is this with agony in His eyes?
- Who is this who is dying on an old, rugged cross?

In reply, the heavens declare:

- He is Jesus—the One who existed with the Father from eternity.
- He is Jesus—the One who spoke, and worlds came into existence.
- He is Jesus—the Divine Son of God.
- He is Jesus—the One at whose

command angels wing their way to worlds afar.

- He is Jesus—the One who died for you and me!
- He is Jesus—the One at whose very name angels break forth in spontaneous song singing, "Holy, holy, holy."

The religious leaders claimed that if Jesus came down from the cross, they would believe in Him. In fact,

Those who in derision uttered the words, "He trusted in God; let Him deliver Him now, if He will have Him: for He said, I am the Son of God," little thought that their testimony would sound down the ages. But although spoken in mockery, these words led men to search the Scriptures as they had never done before. Wise men heard, searched, pondered, and prayed. There were those who never rested until, by comparing scripture with scripture, they saw the meaning of Christ's mission. Never before was there such a general knowledge of Jesus as when He hung upon the cross. Into the hearts of many who beheld the crucifixion scene, and who heard Christ's words, the light of truth was shining.[7]

Jesus' triumph in death

Even while dying, Jesus drew people to Himself. The dying thief hanging on the cross beside Him pled for mercy. He was convicted by the Holy Spirit that Jesus was divine. With intense earnestness, he said, "Lord, remember me when You come into Your kingdom" (Luke 23:42).

Although Jesus was writhing in agony,

dying on the cross, He gave the thief the assurance of eternal life. "And Jesus said to him, 'Assuredly, I say to you, today you will be with Me in Paradise' " (verse 43). The book *The Desire of Ages* gives us some insight into the thief's background:

This man was not a hardened criminal; he had been led astray by evil associations. . . . He had seen and heard Jesus, and had been convicted by His teaching, but he had been turned away from Him by the priests and rulers. Seeking to stifle conviction, he had plunged deeper and deeper into sin, until he was arrested, tried as a criminal, and condemned on the cross. In the judgment hall and on the way to Calvary he had been in company with Jesus. . . . The conviction comes back to him that this is the Christ. . . .

. . . He has seen and read the title above the Saviour's head. . . . The Holy Spirit illuminates his mind, and little by little the chain of evidence is joined together. In Jesus, bruised, mocked, and hanging upon the cross, he sees the Lamb of God, that taketh away the sin of the world.[8]

The appeal of this penitent thief demonstrated that Christ's mission would be successful. The thief's response gave Jesus a glimmer of hope in His darkest hour. Breathing his last, the thief grasped the words of Christ and believed. The thief's acceptance of the gift of eternal life demonstrated before the entire universe that no man on earth and no power of hell could rob Christ of His power to save.

They may strip from Him His raiment, and quarrel over its division. But they cannot rob Him of His power to forgive sins. In dying He bears testimony to His own divinity and to the glory of the Father. . . .

I say unto thee today, Thou shalt be with Me in Paradise. Christ did not promise that the thief should be with Him in Paradise that day. He Himself did not go that day to Paradise. He slept in the tomb, and on the morning of the resurrection He said, "I am not yet ascended to My Father." John 20:17. But on the day of the crucifixion, the day of apparent defeat and darkness, the promise was given. "Today" while dying upon the cross as a malefactor, Christ assures the poor sinner, Thou shalt be with Me in Paradise.[9]

In his life's final moments, the thief on the cross believed in Jesus as the world's Savior and was forgiven. His forgiveness is an invitation for all to come and receive the gift of salvation from Jesus. The thief deserved eternal death, but Jesus offered him eternal life, and he accepted it.

QUESTION **3** What was the purpose of Jesus' death, and why was it so necessary?

But we see Jesus, who was made a little lower than the angels, for the suffering of death crowned with glory and honor, that He, by the grace of God, might taste death for everyone.

For it was fitting for Him, for whom are all things and by whom are all things, in bringing many sons to glory, to make the captain of their salvation perfect through sufferings. . . .

Inasmuch then as the children have partaken of flesh and blood, He Himself likewise shared in the same, that through death He might destroy him who had the power of death, that is, the devil, and release those who through fear of death were all their lifetime subject to bondage (Hebrews 2:9–15).

As a result of sin, we all deserve to die, but Jesus' sacrificial death on the cross has destroyed the power of death. The Scriptures teach that "all have sinned and fall short of the glory of God" (Romans 3:23). Sin's penalty is eternal death. The Bible declares, "For the wages of sin is death, but the gift of God is eternal life in Christ Jesus our Lord" (Romans 6:23). Therefore, Jesus needed to pay the price for our sins. As by faith we accept His great sacrifice, we have eternal life.

When Christ died on Calvary's cross, He willingly assumed all the guilt of our sins. As the divine Son of God, He is our loving Redeemer. Indeed, "Christ was treated as we deserve, that we might be treated as He deserves. He was condemned for our sins, in which He had no share, that we might be justified by His righteousness, in which we had no share. He suffered the death which was ours, that we might receive the life which was His. 'With His stripes we are healed.' "[10]

Jesus' final words

Just before Jesus breathed His last, He cried, "I thirst!" (John 19:28). It is difficult to imagine that the Author of all Creation—the One who created crystal-clear streams, babbling brooks, and flowing rivers—could possibly be thirsty. In His humanity, Jesus was subject to the same physical, mental, and emotional needs of all humanity. It is amazing to think that Jesus, the Creator of all, voluntarily became subject to hunger and thirst. Yet, He would not place in His body anything that would dull His senses. "To those who suffered death by the cross, it was permitted to give a stupefying potion, to deaden the sense of pain. This was offered to Jesus; but when He had tasted it, He refused it. He would receive nothing that could becloud His mind. His faith must keep fast hold upon God. This was His only strength. To becloud His senses would give Satan an advantage."[11]

There is also a much deeper meaning to the words, "I thirst." Jesus had an unquenchable desire for the salvation of all humanity. He longed for men and women to come to Him to experience salvation. His thirst in His dying hour was for those that He came to save, that they would accept His love, be redeemed by His grace, and live forever in His kingdom.

Dark clouds engulfed Golgotha, but deeper darkness flooded the soul of Jesus. He was in a different position than He had ever been before. The guilt of sin was so great—the weight of transgression so enormous that He did not sense the Father's presence. He cried out in agony, "My God, My God, why have You forsaken Me?" (Matthew 27:46). *The Desire of Ages* describes the scene.

> Now with the terrible weight of guilt He bears, He cannot see the Father's reconciling face. The withdrawal of the divine countenance from the Saviour in this hour of supreme anguish pierced His heart with a sorrow that can never be fully understood by man. So great was this agony that His physical pain was hardly felt.
>
> . . . The Saviour could not see through the portals of the tomb. Hope did not present to Him His coming forth from the grave a conqueror, or tell Him of the Father's acceptance of the sacrifice. He feared that sin was so offensive to God that Their separation was to be eternal. Christ felt the anguish which the sinner will feel when mercy shall no longer plead for the guilty race. It was the sense of sin, bringing the Father's wrath upon Him as man's substitute, that made the cup He drank so bitter, and broke the heart of the Son of God.[12]

QUESTION **4** What was Christ's final plea on the cross?

And when Jesus had cried out with a loud voice, He said, "Father, 'into Your hands I commit My spirit.'" Having said this, He breathed His last (Luke 23:46).

In the final moments of Jesus' life on the cross, He had no visible evidence of the Father's presence. The guilt of the sins of the world was crushing out His life. It was by faith that His last words were: "Father, 'into Your hands I commit My spirit' " (Luke 23:46). Jesus' last words from His dying lips were words of absolute trust. He trusted the Father completely and, "in clear trumpet tones, that seemed to resound throughout creation, Jesus cries, 'It is finished.' 'Father, into Thy hands I commend My spirit.' Luke 23:46."[13] Furthermore,

> a light encircled the cross, and the face of the Saviour shone with a glory like the sun. He then bowed His head upon His breast, and died.
>
> Amid the awful darkness, apparently forsaken of God, Christ had drained the last dregs in the cup of human woe. In those dreadful hours He had relied upon the evidence of His Father's acceptance heretofore given Him. He was acquainted with the character of His Father; He understood His justice, His mercy, and His great love. By faith He rested in Him whom it had ever been His joy to obey. And as in submission He committed Himself to God, the sense of the loss of His Father's favor was withdrawn. By faith, Christ was victor.[14]

What did Jesus mean by His final cry on the cross, "It is finished?" There is a richness in this expression, "It is finished." We might ask, What was finished? There are three aspects to this expression:

❶ The plan of salvation was complete. Jesus had accomplished His mission. Eternal life was available to all.

❷ Christ's demonstration of the love of God was finished. In His life and death, He revealed the illimitable, exhaustless love of God.

❸ Death was defeated. Through the cross, death could no longer hold its victims captive. Christ experienced death for all humanity.

In addition,

> it was the marvel of all the universe that Christ should humble Himself to save fallen man. That He who had passed from star to star, from world to world, superintending all, by His providence supplying the needs of every order of being in His vast creation—that He should consent to leave His glory and take upon Himself human nature, was a mystery which the sinless intelligences of other worlds desired to understand. When Christ came to our world in the form of humanity, all were intensely interested in following Him as He traversed, step by step, the bloodstained path from the manger to Calvary. Heaven marked the insult and mockery that He received, and knew that it was at Satan's instigation. They marked the work of counteragencies going forward; Satan constantly pressing darkness, sorrow, and suffering upon the race, and Christ counteracting it. They watched the battle between light and darkness as it waxed stronger.[15]

Jesus' final "It is finished" at the end of time

These words, "It is finished," will echo through the universe one last time. One day soon, the

controversy between good and evil, between Christ and Satan, will finally be finished. The forces of darkness will finally be destroyed. The powers of evil will finally be overcome. Satan and his evil angels will finally be defeated.

Revelation 16:17 declares, "Then the seventh angel poured out his bowl into the air, and a loud voice came out of the temple of heaven, from the throne, saying, 'It is done!'" Essentially, the angel is echoing Jesus' cry, "It is finished." Probation has closed. Every person on planet Earth has made their final, irrevocable decision for or against Christ. Six of the seven last plagues have been poured out. There is devastation everywhere.

The devil has had his day. Now it is God's turn. This divine announcement is followed by flashes of lightning, loud thunder, an earthquake, and huge hailstones falling from heaven. The beast and the powers of evil are defeated. Jesus returns as King of kings and Lord of lords. The armies of heaven totally

defeat Satan and the forces of darkness (see Revelation 19:11–20). Ellen White describes the scene in *The Great Controversy Between Christ and Satan*:

It is at midnight that God manifests His power for the deliverance of His people. The sun appears, shining in its strength. Signs and wonders follow in quick succession. The wicked look with terror and amazement upon the scene, while the righteous behold with solemn joy the tokens of their deliverance. Everything in nature seems turned out of its course. The streams cease to flow. Dark, heavy clouds come up and clash against each other. In the midst of the angry heavens is one clear space of indescribable glory, whence comes the voice of God like the sound of many waters, saying: "It is done." Revelation 16:17.[16]

In addition,

> The voice of God is heard from heaven, declaring the day and hour of Jesus' coming, and delivering the everlasting covenant to His people. . . . Soon there appears in the east a small black cloud, about half the size of a man's hand. It is the cloud which surrounds the Saviour and which seems in the distance to be shrouded in darkness. The people of God know this to be the sign of the Son of man. In solemn silence they gaze upon it as it draws nearer the earth, becoming lighter and more glorious, until it is a great white cloud, its base a glory like consuming fire, and above it the rainbow of the covenant. Jesus rides forth as a mighty conqueror.[17]

In one final, triumphant note, heaven's divine announcement is decreed. The victory that Jesus achieved on the cross when He cried, "It is finished," is now fully realized with the final defeat of all evil. The "it is finished" statement from the cross is the very basis for the cry of "It is finished" at the end time, when Jesus returns a second time. Love has won. Hate has lost. It is finished—the battle is over!

Hunger and heartache are over. Disaster, disease, and death are over. Poverty and pain are over. Sickness, sorrow, and suffering are over. Tears and turmoil are over. War, weariness, and worry are over. Christ's victory on Calvary is the assurance that, one day, every vestige of evil will be defeated forever. It is heaven's eternal pledge that righteousness will triumph over unrighteousness, the truth will triumph over falsehood, and Christ will triumph over Satan. The cross makes it all possible. On an old, rugged cross on a dirt hill outside of Jerusalem, the Son of God died on a Friday. It was a dark, dark Friday. But Resurrection morning was coming. Beyond the rejection and betrayal and despair, beyond the blood, agony, and tears, beyond the brokenness and disappointment, was Resurrection morning.

Jesus' death was required in order to reconcile the gulf between God and man. "For when we were enemies we were reconciled to God through the death of His Son, much more, having been reconciled, we shall be saved by His life" (Romans 5:10).

Sin separates us from God. The only way to bridge the gulf between God and man is through Jesus' great sacrifice in the plan of salvation. Through Jesus Christ, we are reunited with God. Praise His holy name! There is a way of escape for this sinful world. "It was Satan's purpose to bring about an eternal separation between God and man; but in Christ we become more closely united to God than if we had never fallen. In taking our nature, the Saviour has bound Himself to humanity by a tie that is never to be broken. Through the eternal ages, He is linked with us."[18]

The nature of the Godhead—the Father, Son, and Holy Spirit—is love. Because the Father loves us so much, He gave His only begotten Son to die for us (John 3:16). Jesus loves us so much, He would not leave us to perish without hope, and so He took the penalty of sin upon Himself. The Holy Spirit loves us so much that He would not leave us alone but would comfort us.

QUESTION **5** What effect did Christ's death on the cross have upon Satan?

Jesus answered and said, "This voice did not come because of Me, but for your sake. Now is the judgment of this world; now the ruler of this world will be cast out" (John 12:30, 31).

Then I heard a loud voice saying in heaven, "Now salvation, and strength, and the kingdom of our God, and the power of His Christ have come, for the accuser of our brethren, who accused them before our God day and night, has been cast down" (Revelation 12:10).

At the death of Christ, Satan's destruction was assured. As Jesus clearly stated in John 12:31, "Now the ruler of this world will be cast out." The apostle John adds, "For the accuser of our brethren, who accused them before our God day and night, has been cast down" (Revelation 12:10). On the cross, Jesus struck the death knell for Satan's purposes and plans. "Satan saw that his disguise was torn away. His administration was laid open before the unfallen angels and before the heavenly universe. He had revealed himself as a murderer. By shedding the blood of the Son of God, he had uprooted himself from the sympathies of the heavenly beings. Henceforth his work was restricted. . . . The last link of sympathy between Satan and the heavenly world was broken."[19]

Jesus wins! Satan loses! Sin will never raise its ugly head ever again, "What do you conspire against the LORD? He will make an utter end of it. Affliction will not rise up a second time" (Nahum 1:9).

Jesus went through the most difficult experience that anyone will ever have to experience so we could be saved eternally. But it will never happen again. Sin will be no more; it will never rise again. "Through Christ's

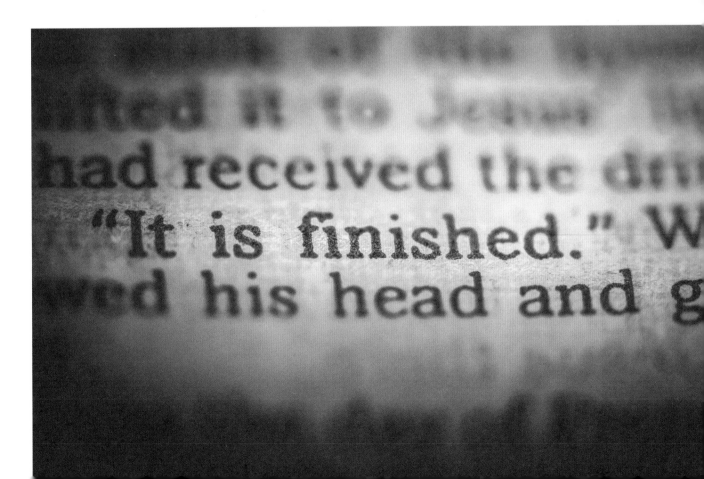

redeeming work the government of God stands justified. The Omnipotent One is made known as the God of love. Satan's charges are refuted, and his character unveiled. Rebellion can never again arise. Sin can never again enter the universe. Through eternal ages all are secure from apostasy. By love's self-sacrifice, the inhabitants of earth and heaven are bound to their Creator in bonds of indissoluble union."[20] Praise God for Jesus and His great sacrifice on Calvary!

Contemplating the life of Christ and accepting Him in our lives daily is what changes us. His grace breaks our hearts. His grace pardons our sins. His grace empowers us to live new lives now and forever. His grace will lead us home so that one day we too can say with Jesus, thank God, "It is finished."

Would you like to open your heart and make a deeper commitment to Jesus? If so, check the appropriate boxes below:

☐ I accept Jesus' great sacrifice on the cross and desire to be ready when He says the last "It is finished" at the end of time.

☐ Although I am committed to Jesus Christ, I sense the need for a new experience with Him.

☐ I once accepted Jesus—but have been away. Now, I desire to come back to Him.

☐ I have never fully received Jesus, but now I choose to accept Him into my life.

☐ I choose to spend more time sharing Jesus Christ with others.

1. Ellen G. White, *The Desire of Ages* (Nampa, ID: Pacific Press®, 2005), 744.
2. White, 744.
3. White, 744.
4. White, 745.
5. White, 745.
6. White, 745, 746.
7. White, 749.
8. White, 749, 750.
9. White, 751.
10. White, 25.
11. White, 746.
12. White, 753.
13. Ellen G. White, *The Story of Redemption* (Washington, DC: Review and Herald®, 1980), 226.
14. White, *Desire of Ages*, 756.
15. Ellen G. White, *Patriarchs and Prophets* (Nampa, ID: Pacific Press®, 2005), 69.
16. Ellen G. White, *The Great Controversy Between Christ and Satan* (Nampa, ID: Pacific Press®, 2005), 636.
17. White, 640, 641.
18. White, *Desire of Ages*, 25.
19. White, 761.
20. White, 26.

NOTES

NOTES